# UNDERSTANDING YOURSELF & OTHERS

## By Bill Riedler

Published by
### GLOBAL

tm

**Relationship
Centers, Inc.**
16101 Stewart Road
Austin, Texas 78734

UNDERSTANDING YOURSELF & OTHERS

# GLOBAL

tm

**Relationship
Centers, Inc.**
16101 Stewart Road
Austin, Texas 78734

Library of Congress Catalog Card Number

82-050460

ISBN 0-933450-01-X

# GLOBAL

tm

**Relationship
Centers, Inc.**

This book is dedicated to all who strive to enjoy rich personal and business relationships.

Bill Riedler

# Global Relationship Centers

tm

# *Table Of Contents*

tm

# *Acknowledgments*

The psychological theory represented in this book is that of Dr. Alfred Adler. Our thinking has been strongly influenced by Rudolf Dreikurs, M.D., who devoted his life to the task of showing others the usefulness of Adlerian psychology.

Appreciation is due to Kath Kvols, Owner of the International Network for Children and Famlies and author of the book, Redirecting Children's Misbehavior, for her extensive assistance in writing this book.

I wish to acknowledge Kurt Adler, Ph.D., M.D.; Harold Mosak, Ph.D.; William Pew, M.D.; Miriam Pew, M.S.W.; Bernard Shulman, M.D.; Robert Powers, B.D., M.A.; and my colleagues at the Global Relationship Centers, who have also stimulated our thinking.

I wish to give thanks to Terri Lash, Sharon and Tenny Lode and Marilyn Ellinghaus for their assistance and for the encouragement they have given us in sharing our work. To Bill Wiley and Mary Ann Fitzharris for the photography.

A special thanks to the many people who have taken our classes and shared their experiences providing us with the examples for this book.

tm

# *Preface*

Where did we get our understanding of people, and most important, our understanding of ourselves? For most of us it was an independent, unsupervised self study program that we, ourselves, organized and implemented when we were between the ages of zero to seven years old. (Most professionals feel that an individual's personality is formed, at least, by age seven.)

Surprisingly, when our understanding of ourselves and others proves to be inadequate for solving the challenges we face, instead of doing something to improve our understanding, we often attempt to solve the problem by putting distance between ourselves and others. We tolerate the discomfort of loneliness and the lack of intimacy because we are unsure of how we can get along comfortably while maintaining our closeness to others.

It is as if we see only two alternatives, each with its unpleasant counterpart. Be close to others and tolerate the restrictions, or be free and tolerate the loneliness. We need something to challenge us at these times when our thinking is so limited, and it is our hope that this book will challenge your thinking as much as Adlerian psychology has challenged ours.

I have found that this information can be used to improve

everyday interactions with people. It helps to improve relationships with the other sex. It is a guide for getting along better with friends and it can be a tool for getting more satisfaction from the work you do. It is an invaluable aid in conflict solving. It will increase your ability to promote mutual agreement and can be used to win people to your way of thinking. Most importantly, this information can help you to find peace and satisfaction in living in a world WITH other people, so you won't have to pay the price of loneliness. It will give you the freedom you have when you are alone, while enriching your life through intimate participation with others.

You will be able to be ALONE/TOGETHER.

Bill Riedler

# *Chapter One*

tm

# THE NEED FOR COURAGE

**How You Developed Your Self-Concept**

When you were a small, helpless infant you were already in the process of developing your self-concept. In order to cope with the uncertainty of your new world you were asking yourself questions such as, *"What am I like?... What are others like?... What can I expect from them and myself?..."* At that very time, everyone else in your world was bigger, more competent and more capable than you. It is most likely that, from that posture of disadvantage, you estimated your abilities and concluded that you had few. At that time your estimate was very accurate. Those early opinions are no longer accurate. However, we all tend to cherish and maintain them, even though we are no longer helpless children. We would suggest that you challenge those opinions that you have made regarding your value, your talents, and your abilities.

## What Are Your Yellow Ropes?

One exercise that we often use in the classes we teach demonstrates how we have all been inadvertently programmed to underestimate ourselves.

We ask a person, let's call her Mary, to put on a belt to which are attached four long yellow ropes. We have other people stand in each of the four corners of the room, each person holding the end of one of the yellow ropes. We blindfold Mary, and place three small objects on the floor, each object in a different location.

Mary is then instructed that her task is to find and pick up the three objects as fast as possible. We explain that the four people holding her yellow ropes want her to succeed. Since she is unable to see well enough on her own, they will use the ropes to guide her.

Then, by gently tugging on her ropes they guide Mary toward the first object. Mary gropes around the floor and finds the first object. Then the guides tug on her ropes again, leading her to the second object. Then the third. Success! The group applauds.

Then we remove Mary's blindfold and place blindfolds on the four people holding Mary's ropes. We give Mary new instructions, telling her to pick up the three objects again. We also stress to Mary *"There are no limitations. You can do anything you want."*

We have performed this demonstration hundreds of times and each time the person wearing the belt reacts in the same way. They either TALK or TUG!

Why don't they ever remove the yellow ropes? The ropes are no longer guidelines, they have become limitations. They paralyze the person wearing the belt. They limit her movement and keep her from success. Yet the person does not take off the belt, she talks, telling the others to *"Pull me this way... You, in the blue shirt, let loose of that rope!"* Or she tugs, trying to overpower those holding her ropes.

## We Are Programmed To Underestimate Ourselves
In a few short minutes, Mary was programmed to underestimate herself and overestimate what she needed from others. She was programmed to be dependent on those yellow ropes even though she was no longer blindfolded!

Let's explore what made that happen. Her opinion of the situation was formed when she was limited. When she needed the others because she could not see. Later, when her own abilities had increased and the others were no longer interested in her success, Mary still maintained the opinion she had formed earlier. The opinion that OTHER PEOPLE determine her destiny.

Where are your yellow ropes? Who or what is holding you back? Do you really need to control them or wait for them to take action before you can make your life the way you want it to be? What would happen if you took off those ropes? Do you really still need that much guidance? Would they still resist you if you took kind but firm, considerate action? The following is an example of how a husband took off those yellow ropes.

*Sue and Tom had come to us for marriage counseling. Tom's complaint was that Sue would lose her temper and holler at him. He would tell her to "stop yelling" but that would make her even more angry.*

Tom was underestimating himself. He was concentrating on what he had to make HER do and he was overlooking what HE could do.

*We asked Tom if he had any idea of what he was doing wrong. He told us that sometimes she talks to him in a quiet voice first and that he sometimes doesn't respond with as much interest as she would like him to. But he still felt that was no reason for her to holler at him.*

We helped him recognize what HE could do.

*In our next session, he reported that Sue had started to holler at him about never wanting to go out in the evenings. He immediately walked up to her with a friendly look on his face.*

Getting close makes it very difficult for the other person to holler.

*In a very calm voice he said, "Sue, I can understand that I make you feel like hollering when I act like I'm not interested in what you are saying. I think I did it because I'd rather just be home alone with you and I felt uncomfortable telling you that.. Instead of fighting, let's work it out. " Sue said it made her stop yelling and she even felt foolish for being so unreasonable.*

Tom discovered that he doesn't need to tell Sue to stop yelling. If he doesn't like yelling, he now realizes that HE can do things to stop it.

Remember, concentrate on what YOU can do.

## Controlling Nature

One of our colleagues tells a story of how he used the same method to control the setting of the sun.

*When he first moved to Colorado, he was anxious to see one of the beautiful mountain sunsets. He went to the top of one of the mountains and waited for the sun to go down. It took longer than he anticipated and he began to get chilly. He became irritated that the sun wasn't setting faster. Then he contemplated what he could do. He discovered that by walking back down the mountain he could change his perspective, and PRESTO! the sun went down.*

We can have a tremendous influence on any situation when we stop trying to control others and concentrate on what WE can do.

## Should Life Be Your Way?

No one in the world has experienced the pain that you have experienced. Or the joy. No one else has your unique collection of strong points and weak points. No other person has experienced your complete set of failures and successes. You are one of a kind and only you can see the world from your perspective. No one else can stand in the exact same place that you are standing. Only you can see life from where you are. You are unique.

Along with this uniqueness comes an obligation. Only you know what this world needs from your perspective. If you don't contribute to improve upon the problems you are aware of, then others will have to tolerate those problems whenever they happen to be in that space.

Not only should life be your way, but you have an obligation to make it happen your way. Fulfilling this obligation provides a deep satisfaction - the feeling of being worthwhile. It is what Alfred Adler called social interest.

19

If we each develop the courage to do what we can to improve upon the problems we see, then we, as a group, will have made this planet a better place for ourselves and others.

Our uniqueness can be our guide, unless we surrender it by trying to be "normal." When we become over-concerned about being "normal" it is like putting on a uniform so that we are identical to all the others. We become predictable and easy to control. We lose that feeling of satisfaction and become over concerned with the task of proving ourselves. To protect our fragile status we desperately try to avoid making mistakes.

Avoiding pain, mistakes or problems is not essential. In fact, pain, mistakes, and problems can be our best indicators, showing us what we can do to become more effective contributors. They can be used as tools to help us increase our social interest.

Studies have shown that the majority of doctors and others who have dedicated themselves to the medical field have early memories of death, illness or injury. These early life catastrophes were the very things that motivated them to endure the difficult tasks of preparing for a career in the medical field. As children they looked at these difficulties and concluded, *"Life is dangerous. You can get sick, hurt or die. I must fight sickness and death!"*

Others, however, who also have similar early memories do not become doctors or nurses. They see the same sickness, injury and death but come to a different conclusion *"Life is dangerous. You could get sick and die! I am afraid. I must avoid life!"* These people may become hypochondriacs.

The difference is their level of courage. With courage, every problem becomes an opportunity. One of our biggest tasks in life is to keep ourselves encouraged.

It is very tempting to indulge ourselves in discouragement. We do it by concentrating on what we can't do, what won't work, what is wrong and how futile it would be to strive to change or improve things. We create the feelings of "Who cares" or "What's the use." We can then use these feelings to justify our decision to give up.

What are the privileges of giving up? We don't need to worry about failing or making mistakes. We don't need to risk finding out if we really can do whatever it was that we were attempting to do.

Giving up, however, also has a price. We miss out on the joy of success. We miss out on the chance to learn from our mistakes. As a result, we never get a chance to discover our true limits and we pass up opportunities to feel worthwhile.

If Mary chooses to never remove her yellow ropes, she can continue to blame her failures on the people holding her ropes. However, if she builds her courage and removes the ropes, she can find out just how capable she is. Then she can work on improving her skill.

We had a client who complained, *"I don't enjoy my time after work."* We asked her what she did and she stated that she always stayed home. When asked why, she explained, *"If I go out I may have a lousy time.""* Her logic expresses her discouragement and her lack of confidence in her abilities. *"I 'm staying home and having a lousy time because if I go out I may have a lousy time!"*

To achieve the satisfaction she desires she must start by re-assessing her own abilities. She must reconsider the impact she has on others and recognize how much she influences the way the world treats her.

## You Change The World
It is easy to underestimate our impact on the world. We seem so small and insignificant compared to the vastness

of the universe. We need to frequently reestablish a feeling of worth.

Consider your activities yesterday. Who did you influence? Who did you influence indirectly? Most of the time we do not even hear about the effects of our interactions with others. For example, I received the following letter from a woman in Texas who had read our book on parenting:

*Dear Bill,*

*I wanted to write to you and tell you what a difference your book has made in my life....*

The letter went on to explain how she used the book to get her two children to behave better.

*In the last week I've applied the theory on my children, and, will wonders never cease, for the first time in 10 years haven't screamed, cried, pounded, spanked, threatened or punished.*

*Suddenly my children, both whom I thought of as headstrong, independent, selfish, etc. (though they were pretty' good, I must admit) have suddenly become cooperative, helpful, willing, sharing, etc., etc.*

The letter showed that we obviously influenced her life and even the lives of her children. However, my point is not the influence that I had on her, but the influence that she had on me.

On the day I received the letter I was in the midst of a very busy schedule preparing to leave the following week on a speaking tour. I had written the basic parts of this book eight months earlier, but the manuscript was in need of reorganizing. I had been putting it off for quite some time. It was her letter that inspired me to make room in a very busy schedule to complete the manuscript.

22

If it wasn't for her decision to write to me, you may not have had the opportunity to read this book now. It may have still been sitting in my "things to be done" pile.

I doubt if the woman in Texas is even aware of the number of people she is influencing every day whenever someone reads this book.

Who are you indirectly influencing? When you spent that dollar yesterday for lunch what impact did that have on the economy? Part of the money you spent on purchasing this book goes to us and enables us to write and lecture more. You then get part credit for every lecture we present.

Were you friendly to a stranger? What effect may that have had on the decisions he made that day? Did you decide to get married, change jobs, move? Think of how many different people will be affected by your decisions. What would have been different in your partner's life if you had not developed the courage to get married?

Occasionally, we are tempted to feel, *"The world would be better off without me."* There is a movie called "IT'S A WONDERFUL LIFE" that graphically shows the fallacy in this type of negative thinking. The main character in the movie (Jimmy Stewart) has several discouraging experiences and decides to commit suicide. An angel comes down from heaven and tries to talk him out of killing himself but the main character says, *"The world would have been better off without me."* The angel takes him back to his home town and shows him what it would have been like had he never been alive. Everything is different! Even the name of the town. Many people are no longer living because of the lack of his efforts. One lady had become a prostitute because she had not received his encouragement and assistance. Needless to say, when he sees how much of a positive difference his life makes, he decides to continue living.

You are a tremendous force for good in this world. Every movement you make spreads out like waves from a pebble dropped into a pond. It is your task to keep yourself encouraged. Understanding yourself and others better is the first step in improving your self-concept. Perhaps by sharing our training and work with you we can improve our understanding of each other.

### How To Encourage Yourself

In the following chapters we are going to present material that will help you become a more responsible individual. Taking on that responsibility will give you tremendous control over your life. Whenever you claim that you are not responsible you are denying your ability to change the situation. At that point you are concentrating on all the things you cannot control. However, the minute you accept responsibility you start concentrating on the things that you can control. This allows you to be effective. To be able to take on this responsibility you must first be encouraged.

With all the challenges that life presents to you it is extremely important that you take responsibility for keeping yourself encouraged. That is your most important task. Many have talked about self-confidence as if it is some inborn quality that a person either possesses or doesn't possess. An individual's self-confidence is constantly varying, based upon his decision to encourage or discourage himself at any given moment.

### The Self-Confidence Test

This is a test that you can perform several times during the day. It will tell you your level of self-confidence.

To start the test, let your mind wander. Do it now, for about 60 seconds. Then read on.

Were you thinking thoughts that encouraged you or thoughts that were discouraging? If you discovered that you were discouraging yourself ask, *"Why might I want to be discouraged right now? Why may I be trying to lower my level of confidence? Is there some task that I wish to avoid? Why am I not motivating myself?"*

Now let your mind wander again. Only, this time, encourage Yourself. Enjoy the beauty of some of the simple things around you. Enjoy the feel of the air as you breathe in. Explore the intricacy of the things that you see. Look with amazement at the wonder of how your eyes work. If you don't have eyesight then explore the wonder of how you have compensated by using your sense of touch. Next, listen to all the sounds you can hear. Enjoy them. Now start considering some of your accomplishments. They don't have to be big accomplishments. Do it now before reading on.

There are two ways that you may have responded to this exercise. You may have redirected your concerns from the goal of proving yourself to the goal of enjoying life. Just making that simple switch in your goals will raise your level of self-confidence. Or, you may have caught your thoughts drifting to what you have not yet accomplished and found it difficult to switch back to enjoying the moment.

If you caught yourself thinking such things such as, "Who cares?" or "I haven't accomplished anything" then you are probably determined to discourage yourself.

Creating an "I don't care" attitude is a way to rationalize your choice to give up. Dissipating courage is the first step of giving up. Your thoughts are the early stages of the action you plan to take. You now know something that you didn't know before - that you are working very hard to fool yourself into believing that you are justified in giving up. Use this information to re-evaluate your decision. You may still give up if you wish to, but you no longer need to go to all the trouble of deceiving yourself.

## Encouraging Others
You can also increase your self-confidence by encouraging others. Taking a moment to turn your eyes outward by becoming interested in another person prevents us from

saying, *"woe is me."* Unfortunately, we have not been trained to encourage others. Because our status has traditionally been measured by comparison to others, most of us are more interested in keeping others down.

Notice that we seldom build monuments or name streets to honor an individual until after he is dead. It is as if we feel, *"I better not give him too much encouragement while he is alive or that S.O.B. might get inspired and out-do me."* When we are only concerned with being helpful and improving the situation then our status is not threatened and we can cooperate.


### Putting Others Down

Did you ever consider that every time you talk critically about another person you are discouraging yourself? And, the person you are talking to wonders what critical things you will be saying to others about him. You are communicating to your friend, *"You had better not allow me to see any of your shortcomings or I will reveal them to others."* This deteriorates the level of trust between you and your friend and prevents closeness and intimacy.

Conversely, discussing what you appreciate about others builds your courage and motivates the person you are talking with.

When I was just out of high school I took a public speaking class. One day I arrived early and was talking to the instructor. He said, *"I was teaching a class last night and one of the speakers picked up a tray and slammed it on the floor. Everyone in the room stopped talking and stared at him. Then the speaker told the group that he had slammed the tray because what he was now going to say was very important and he wanted their undivided attention."* The instructor continued telling me how impressed he was that the speaker was so effective.

The fact that the instructor told me that story changed my life. I decided right then that I, too, wanted to become an effective speaker. Perhaps, if the instructor had told me a story about how someone had made a really bad speech I may have avoided becoming a professional lecturer.

Try it. Tell one of your friends about how impressed you are with someone.

## Is Life A Joke?

Another way to encourage yourself is to recognize when you are taking life too seriously. Remember, no one actually knows what life is really about. Whenever we recognize that we are taking life too seriously we joke and say, *"Wouldn't it be funny if science suddenly discovered that everything is predetermined?""* Or, *"suppose we Discovered that the Earth is only a toy in some giant's pocket."* The joke would then be on us. How seriously we take things! Why not just relax and see what happens, doing whatever we can without condemning ourselves?

This relaxed attitude helps us keep things in perspective. Who knows? Maybe nothing can be changed. However, since we don't really know, it is to our advantage to look at things as if we can change everything. Then we are sure not to pass up any opportunities to improve upon what can be changed. At the same time we must avoid condemning ourselves for our failure to change things. Humor allows us to take all the responsibility without overwhelming ourselves with guilt.

## Fear Of Mistakes

Our ability to encourage ourselves is also limited because we tend to fear making mistakes. Let's explore some of the problems we cause ourselves when we don't develop enough courage to allow ourselves to make mistakes.

A mother who had come to us for family counseling was complaining that she was frequently irritable and grouchy with her husband and children. We discovered that she was a Perfectionist. We asked her, *"How many mistakes will you allow yourself to make each day?"* Her answer suggested that she felt mistakes were bad and should be avoided at all costs. We convinced her to allow herself to make fifty mistakes per day. If she made more than that we would give her permission to condemn herself.

She returned the next week and reported that she had not been grouchy all week. *"And I never made more than five or six mistakes per day!"* she exclaimed.

## Hiding Our Mistakes

The lack of the courage to be imperfect is one of the major deterrents to mental health. We all make mistakes. However, when we feel the need to be perfect we abdicate responsibility for our errors by the use of many neurotic, and in some cases psychotic, evasive maneuvers.

Here is how it is done. We erase awareness of our own mischief from our consciousness and instead we turn our attention toward the things that everyone else is doing wrong. In so doing it becomes impossible for us to see what we are doing wrong. By concentrating only on what others should do we overlook what we can do to improve upon the situation. Our lack of awareness also causes us to feel out of control, as if we didn't possess the skills to avoid the problems confronting us. This adds to our sense of discouragement and to our feelings of inadequacy. We attempt to compensate by trying even harder to disguise our mistakes. We create brilliant rationalizations and explanations to justify our mistakes. *"The only reason I got a speeding ticket is because everyone else was speeding and I didn't want to impede traffic. Besides, the police shouldn't be using those radar traps anyway."* These justifications only perpetuate our problems.

## The Courage To Be Imperfect

The solution to this dilemma is to develop the courage to be imperfect. One of the privileges of being human is that we have the right to be imperfect. Many times, however, we refuse to accept this right. Not that any of us are ever perfect, because we all make many, many mistakes every day, but we often attempt to disguise those mistakes from both ourselves and others. If we had the courage to be imperfect we could become aware of our mistakes and then recognize how to change our behavior.

Once while attending one of Dr. Dreikurs' workshops his wife, Sadie Dreikurs, who was always aware of what the audience needed to hear, said to him, *"Tell them about the feeling of being awed by the power of waterfalls."*

Reprinted here, with Sadie's permission are parts of that now famous speech, "The Courage to be Imperfect." We feel that it is such an important document that it should be read by everyone.

# The Courage To Be Imperfect

### From a Speech by
### Rudolf Dreikurs, M.D.

I have chosen today only one aspect of psychological importance to present to you for your thought and consideration; the subject of *"The Courage to be Imperfect."*

I have found many, many people who try so hard to be good. But I have failed yet to see that they have done so for the welfare of others. What I find behind these people who try to be so good is a concern with their own prestige. They are good for the benefit of their own self elevation. Anybody who is really concerned with the welfare of others won't have any time or interest to become concerned with the question of how good he is. To explain a little bit further I might perhaps present to you two ways of moving on the social scene; two ways of working, of applying oneself. We can distinguish them as the horizontal plane and the vertical plane. What do I mean by that? Some people entirely and others in certain areas move on the horizontal plane. That means that whatever they do they move toward others. They want to do something for others, they are interested in others - they merely function. That is clearly distinguishable from another motivation by which people move on the vertical plane. Whatever they are doing, they are doing it because they want to be higher, they want to be better.

As a matter of fact, improvement and contributions can be done in either way. There are people who do something well because they enjoy doing it, and others who can do something well because they are so glad to prove how good they are. Even human progress probably depends just as well on the contributions of those who move on the horizontal and on the vertical plane. Many have done tremendous benefit to mankind actually motivated only by the question of proving how good they are looking for their own superiority. And others have done a great deal of good - as we call it, in an unselfish way - without consideration of what they may get out of it. And yet there is a fundamental difference in the way things are accomplished: whether you move on the horizontal or the vertical plane you go up, you increase your knowledge, you increase your status, your respect, your prestige - perhaps even your money. But at the same time nobody who moves on the vertical plane is ever only moving up. He is constantly moving up and down, up and down. One day when he does something good he moves a few notches up; next moment when he makes some mistake he moves back down again. Up and down, up and down. That is exactly the plane on which most of our contemporaries move today. The consequences are obvious. A person who moves on the vertical plane can never be sure that he is high enough, never be sure the next morning that he is not coming down again. Therefore he has to live with tension and fears and anxieties. He is constantly vulnerable. As soon as something doesn't go well, down he goes - if not in the opinion of others, then in his own.

Quite different is the movement on the horizontal plane. The person who moves on the horizontal plane is constantly moving ahead in the direction he wants to move. He doesn't move up but he moves ahead. When something goes wrong, he considers what's going on, tries to find a way around, tries to remedy it. He is merely motivated by interest. If his motivation is very strong, he may even have enthusiasm. But he doesn't think about his own self elevation; he is interested in functioning instead of being concerned with his status or prestige.

And so we can see how on the one side, on the horizontal plane we have the desire to be useful. On the vertical plane we have the desire for self-elevation with the constant fear of making mistakes. And yet, most people today, stimulated by our general social values of social competition, are entirely devoting themselves to the problem of their own value and self-elevation - never sure that they are good enough, never quite sure that they will measure up; even though in the eyes of their fellow man they may be highly successful.

Now that points us, then, to a crucial question for those who are so concerned with self elevation. The crucial question is the problem of mistakes - making mistakes.

Perhaps we first have to state a little bit clearer why people became concerned - badly concerned - with the danger of making a mistake. We can perhaps refer first to our tradition, to our cultural tradition. In an autocratic society, making a mistake is unpardonable, intolerable. The king, the master, never makes a mistake because he has the right to do as he darn well pleases. And there is nobody who can tell him he has done something wrong, except at the danger of losing his head. Mistakes are only possible to be made by subordinates. The only one who decides whether a mistake is made is the boss.

Making a mistake means thereby nonconformity with the demands: *"As long as you do as I tell you there is no mistake possible because I am right. I say so. Making a mistake therefore means that you don't do what I tell you. And I won't stand for that. If you dare to do something wrong - that means different from what I tell you - you can count on the worst possible punishment. And in case you have any delusion that I might not be able to punish you, there will be somebody higher than me who will see to it that you will be punished. A mistake is a deadly sin. Making a mistake incurs the worst possible fate."* That is a typical and necessary authoritarian concept of cooperation. Cooperation means doing as I tell you.

32

It seems to me that our fear of making a mistake has a different meaning. It is an expression of our highly competitive way of living. Making a mistake becomes so dangerous not because of the punishment - of which we don't think -but because of the lowering of our status, of the ridicule, of the humiliation, which it may incur: "If I do something wrong and you find that I am doing something wrong, then I am no good. And if I am no good, then I have no respect, I have no status. Then you might be better than me." Horrible thought!

"I want to be better than you because I want to be superior." But in our present era we haven't so many other signs of superiority. Now the white man no longer can be so proud of his superiority because he is white; and the man because he is a man and looks down on the women- we can't let him do that anymore. And even the superiority of money is another question because we can lose it. The Great Depression has shown it to us.

There is only one area where we can still feel safely superior: When we are right. It is a new snobbism of intellectuals: "I know more, therefore you are stupid and I am superior to you." And it is in this competitive drive to accomplish a moral and intellectual superiority that making a mistake becomes so dangerous again "If you find out that I am wrong, how can I look down on you? And if I can't look down at you, you certainly can look down at me."

That is how human relations of today are in our community just as much as in our families, where brothers and sisters, husbands and wives, parents and children look down on each other for doing wrong and each one trying to prove so desperately that he is right and the other is wrong Except, those who don't care any more can tell you, "You are right, you think, but I have the power to punish you; I will do what I want, and you can't stop me." But of course, while we feel defeated by a little child who is our boss and who does what he pleases, we still have one thing left: at least we know we are right and he is wrong.

Mistakes present you with a predicament. But if you are not discouraged, if you are willing and able to take and utilize your inner resources, the predicament is only stimulating you to better and more successful efforts. There is no sense in crying over spilled milk.

But most people who make mistakes feel guilty; they feel degraded, they lose respect for themselves, they lose belief in their own ability. And I have seen it time and time again: The real damage was not done through the mistakes they made but through the guilt feeling, discouragement, which they had afterwards. Then they really messed it up for themselves. As long as we are so preoccupied with the fallacious assumption of the importance of mistakes, we can't take mistakes in our stride. And so this mistaken idea of the importance of mistakes leads us to a mistaken concept of ourselves. We become overly impressed by everything that's wrong in us and around us. Because, if I am critical of myself, I naturally am going to be critical of the people around me. If I am sure that I am no good, I have at least to find that you are worse. That is what we are doing. Anyone who is critical of himself is always critical of others.

And so we have to learn to make peace with ourselves as we are. Not, the way many say, *"What are we after all? We are a speck of sand on the beaches of life, we are limited in time and space. We are so small and insignificant. How short is our life, how small and insignificant is our existence. How can we believe in our strength, in our power?"*

When you stand before a huge waterfall, or see a huge snowcapped mountain, or are in a thunderstorm most people are inclined to feel weak and awed, confronted with this majesty and power of nature. And very few people draw the only conclusion which in my mind would be correct: the realization that all of this power of the waterfall, this majesty of the mountain, this tremendous impressiveness of the thunderstorm are part of the same life which is in me. Very few people who stand in awe of this expression of nature stand in awe before themselves, admiring this tremendous organization of their body, their glands, their physiology, this tremendous power of their brain. This self realization of what we are is missing because we are now slowly emerging from a traditional power of autocracy where the masses don't count and only the brains and only the emperor and the divine authority knew what was good for the people. We haven't freed ourselves yet from the slave mentality of an autocratic past.

How many things would be different in everyone's surroundings if we hadn't lived? How a good word may have encouraged some fellow and he did it differently and better than he would have otherwise. And through him somebody else was saved. How much we contribute to each other, how powerful we each are and don't know it. And that is the reason then why we can't be satisfied with ourselves and look to elevate ourselves - afraid of the mistakes which would ruin us - and try desperately to gain the superiority over others. So perfection, therefore, is by no means a necessity; it is even impossible.

There are people who are always so afraid of doing wrong because they don't see their value; remain eternal students because only in school one can tell them what is right, and they know how to get good grades. But in life you can't do that. All the people who are afraid of making mistakes, who want by all means to be right, can't function well. But there is only one condition on which you can be sure you are right when you are trying to do something right. There is one condition alone which would permit you to be relatively sure whether you are right or wrong. That is <u>afterwards</u>. When you do something you never

35

can be sure - you can only see if it is right by how it turns out. Anybody who has to be right can't move much, can't make any decision, because we can never be sure that we are right. To be right is a false premise and it usually leads to the misuse of this right. Have you any idea of the difference between logical right and psychological right? Have you any idea how many people are torturing their friends and their families because they have to be right and unfortunately they are? There is nothing worse than the person who always has the right argument. There is nothing worse than a person who is always right morally. And he shows it.

This right morally and right logically is very often an offense to human relationships. In order to be right you sacrifice kindness, patience if you want, tolerance. No, out of this desire for rightness we don't get peace, we don't get cooperation; we merely end up by trying to give the others the idea of how good we are when we can't even fool ourselves. No, to be human does not mean to be right, does not mean to be perfect. To be human means to be useful, to make contributions, not for oneself, but others; to take what there is and make the best out of it. It requires faith in oneself and faith and respect for others. But that has a prerequisite: That we can't be overly concerned with their shortcomings, because if we are impressed and concerned with their shortcomings, we have no respect, either for ourselves or for others.

We have to learn the art, and to realize that we are good enough as we are because we never will be better, regardless of how much more we may know, how much more skill we may acquire, how much status or money or what-have-you. If we can't make peace with ourselves as we are, we never will be able to make peace with ourselves. And this requires the courage to be imperfect; requires the realization that I am no angel, that I am not super-human, that I make mistakes, that I have faults; but I am pretty good because I don't have to be better than the others. Which is a tremendous belief. If you accept just being yourself, the devil of vanity, the golden calf of "my superiority" vanish. If we learn to function, to do our best regardless of what it is; out of the enjoyment of the functioning we can grow just as well, even better than if we would drive ourselves to be perfect - which we can't be.

We have to learn to live with ourselves and the relationship of natural limitations and the full awareness of our own strengths.

## Mistakes Are Valuable Training Tools

It is not an easy task to develop this courage. To help our clients become more aware of their hesitation to accept their own imperfections we often ask: *"What mistakes will you accept in yourself? Is it all right that you never arranged to get more training in cooperation?"* When we ask this question, occasionally someone will answer, *"Yes."* We then ask, *"Even if that lack of training resulted in your choice to get divorced? Or do you instead, feel your divorce was the result of character flaws in your ex-wife?"*

If we have the courage to be human, then we can look at our own shortcomings and learn and improve. If not we tend to look to others for the blame. Ask yourself, *"Am I learning from my mistakes or am I using them as an excuse to give up?"*

With courage our mistakes become valuable training tools. If we lack that courage, we become defensive and pass up opportunities to learn more about ourselves. The courage to be imperfect allows us to take full responsibility for our actions.

Global Relationship Centers

38

# Chapter Two

tm

## OUR FEELINGS AND EMOTIONS

### Creative Responsibility

Many people fear being responsible. This fear is a symptom showing that they lack the courage to be imperfect. Avoiding responsibility also causes them to lose their personal power. Overcoming your fear of being responsible can be the most important step you ever take. Taking responsibility can be a very enlightening process if we do it without condemning ourselves.

We suggest that instead of saying, *"That's unfair. How come they did that to me?"* You say, *"I must not have protected myself well enough. How can I improve upon that?"* However, in taking total responsibility, it is essential that you do not condemn yourself. You must look at the situation as an adventure. *"Isn't that interesting how I just arranged to get my wife angry by using that tone of voice?"*

39

As opposed to *"OH NO! I did it again! I used the wrong tone of voice. What's wrong with me?"*

With this second response you will only succeed in discouraging yourself. The first response exemplifies what Rudolf Dreikurs called the courage to be imperfect. With this courageous attitude you prepare to take total responsibility for whatever your results happen to be. This will give you a powerful new tool for self-insight.

We call this technique *"creative responsibility"* because whenever we take total responsibility it forces us to think creatively about why we are getting results that are different from what we claim we desire.

As the first step of using *"creative responsibility,"* it will be necessary to re-examine our understanding of feelings and emotions so we can recognize how they are used to move us closer to, or farther from, others. We offer the following glossary:

## GLOSSARY OF FEELINGS & EMOTIONS

### 1. CREATIVE RESPONSIBILITY
Looking at the results you achieve "as if" those were the results you wanted. (Even if you feel that your intentions were different.) Then use this sense of responsibility not to blame yourself or to feel guilty, but to explore creative possibilities as to why you may have wanted the results you achieved.

### 2. FEELINGS
The steam that we create to drive us in the direction that we intend to move.

### 3. SUBCONSCIOUS INTENTIONS
Unadmitted objectives that coincide more with our style of life than with common sense. We don't admit these intentions to ourselves so that we don't have to examine the flaws in our value system. Often we see our value

system or life style as a necessity to survival and often resist revising it. A scuba diver burdened with a tank of bad air may refuse changing tanks under water because he may feel that, *"Bad air is better than no air!"*

## 4. GUILT
A feeling we sometimes create after violating good intentions to help us believe that we really had good intentions. Notice that we seldom feel guilty in time to avoid doing the mischief. We usually feel guilty after the deed is done. It is ironic that we judge others by their actions, but judge ourselves only by our own good intentions. This allows us to misbehave without violating our conscience. Occasionally we even try to convince others of our innocence by expressing how guilty we feel.

## 5. WORRY
Excessive thinking or laboring over a situation instead of taking action. We engage in this activity to avoid doing what we do not feel prepared to do. After a short time of worrying we usually have discouraged ourselves and dissipated our energy. It is a way to feel justified in being unmotivated to take the actions that the situation is demanding. We arrange to worry when we feel unprepared to meet the situation courageously.

Occasionally we worry to gain privileges or to justify hostile action. If we allow someone else to make us worry about them for several hours, then we can feel justified in trying to control them. Example: *"Johny, where have you been? I've been worried sick about you! Just for that, I'm not letting you go to that party tomorrow."*

## 6. JEALOUSY
A feeling we create to control others, maintain their attention, hurt them, or create a distraction so they won't notice our shortcomings.

### 7. DREAMS

The factory of emotions and feelings. A system to assist you in interpreting your dreams will be presented later in this chapter.

### 8. HOSTILE FEELINGS

Thoughts that we dwell upon to help us feel that someone else should take action. We usually create these feelings when life is demanding something of us that is not consistent with our life style.

### 9. ANGER

An attempt to get others to do that which we want them to do by intimidating them. We usually choose this method when we feel powerless. Even though it usually doesn't influence the other person to cooperate, it does give us a sense of our own power.

### 10. SELF ANGER

A feeling created to either make ourselves feel as if we are doing something about a problem, to influence others not to make demands of us, or to motivate ourselves to improve upon the situation.

### 11. TEMPER

Creating a feeling of being out of control when we are trying to scare someone to our way of thinking and we don't wish to take responsibility for our choice of tactics.

### 12. BOREDOM

A way of asking someone else to make life exciting for you or a covert rebellion against life's demands. *"I would do it if it were interesting to me."* A justification for not participating at 100%.

### 13. LOVE

The feelings we create which help us emphasize strong points and overlook weaknesses. We create these feelings AFTER we have chosen to be close, although we sometimes claim that it was the feelings that made us choose. We do this so that we do not feel responsible for the decision. This topic will be discussed in detail in the chapter on "The Other Sex."

## 14. DEPRESSION
A silent temper tantrum.

## EXAMPLES OF GLOSSARY TERMS

Perhaps you don't agree with some of these definitions. That's understandable because these definitions put all of the responsibility right on your own shoulders. Before you discard these definitions read the following examples. You will find that if you use the information described in the examples you will gain a totally new understanding of many of the issues in your personal life that you now see as problems. You will be able to improve the quality of your life.

### CREATIVE RESPONSIBILITY example:
I was hired by a manufacturing company to be in charge of all production. The company was having morale problems and profits were down. The owner felt that my understanding of psychology could help. I worked for the company for ten months and made many improvements and then I was fired. I didn't want to get fired. I, at first, felt that I was the victim of the owner's poor judgment. Then I decided to look at the problem from the point of view of *"creative responsibility."* As if whatever happened was what I wanted to happen. I attempted to rethink the situation to figure out why I may have wanted to get fired.

The situation that led to my being fired was that I wanted to change one of the foreman from hourly pay to a fixed salary. I asked the owner's permission to make the change and he said he wanted to think about it. I continued to press him for his answer. After two weeks of not getting his reply, I told him that I had to know by the end of that day. I still did not get his answer. So, the next morning I made the change without his permission. When he came in that day

I told him that I had made the change. He said that he would have to fire me for acting without his approval.

I could easily justify being fired by saying that the owner was keeping me from doing my job by not making a decision. But, looking at the situation from that point of view wouldn't help me understand myself.

Perhaps I wanted to get fired because we were just arriving at the point where all of my ideas were to be tested. Would they really work? Would morale improve and profits go up? If, after being fired, things did improve, I could claim that the improvements were due to the changes that I had made prior to being fired. If things didn't improve I could claim that it was because the owner fired me before I completed my work. Perhaps getting fired was a way to avoid being tested. Perhaps I allowed it to happen to me or even arranged it because I lacked confidence in my skills.

After recognizing why I may have wanted to get fired, I then went on to figure out how I may have arranged for that to happen. I was fired because I apparently did not have the skills to encourage the owner to make a decision. Could that be true? Hardly! In the ten months of working with him I demonstrated on many occasions that I did have that ability. Many of the foremen would come to me for advice on how they could get the owner's approval. I was an expert on getting him to decide!

In looking more closely at the way I approached him about the decision, I recognized that I had violated all of the principles that I had often suggested to the others. I didn't clearly define the benefits to him. I left him responsible for the results of the decision instead of taking responsibility myself. I wasn't enthusiastic and I didn't present the idea in a way that showed him the situation well enough to assure him that my choice was to his best benefit.

There is no way to be certain that I really wanted to get fired or if I was just the victim. It doesn't matter. I still benefited greatly from my use of creative responsibility.

Afterwards, I felt extremely confident and had learned many new things about myself. I decided not to be afraid of testing my ideas. I persuaded the owner to hire me for another week so that I could write up all the plans that I had in progress. That way he could continue to implement them in my absence. We then parted good friends. The lessons I had learned gave me the courage to open my own business.

**FEELINGS example:**
Jerry had been having an affair and his wife found out about it. She had asked him to choose between her and the other woman. His wife was pregnant at the time and Jerry claimed that he wanted to make the "right" decision, and stay with his wife. BUT! *"My feelings for the other woman are so strong that I may not be able to commit to my wife."*

Jerry was not taking responsibility for his choice to give up his wife and family to go with another woman. He was putting the blame on his feelings so he could do what he wanted to do - ignore the social order and still maintain a good opinion of himself. He had created a brilliant rationale for rejecting his wife. He had *"fallen in love"* with the other woman. Jerry could not be blamed because he *"wanted"* to do the right thing. He was saying, *"I'm innocent. My feelings are guilty."*

**SUBCONSCIOUS INTENTIONS example:**
Betty was the oldest of three children. As a child she often gained more status than her two brothers by saying, *"I'm the oldest and mom told me what she wanted and you shouldn't be doing that."* The boys would then yell at her and call her names. Mom would hear the fight and reprimand the boys. Betty developed the style of, *"I'm important when the others see how right I am."*

Betty came to counseling to complain about how rude her husband was to her. When we asked her to tell us about her memory of the moment she first realized that she was in love with him, she said:

*"It was the moment I first met him. I was in a drugstore and I heard someone yelling at the clerk. I looked over there and saw him. He was so handsome."*

She did not consciously choose a husband who would be willing to be rude to her. She operated on her subconscious intentions. This was a man who would fit well into her plan to convince others of her superiority. By allowing him to be rude to her, Betty could convince all of her friends that her husband was in the wrong.

Betty was not consciously aware of the reasons why she "saw" him as handsome. Her subconscious intentions were aligned with her lifestyle of being right. They did not make common sense.

### GUILT example:

John asked Sue to do a favor for him. He asked her to pick up a legal document because he didn't have time to do it. He agreed to call the lawyer's office to make the necessary arrangements so that the document could legally be picked up by her. John *"forgot"* to make the arrangements. When Sue arrived, the attorney was unwilling to give her the document. Because of John's mistake. Sue had to make two extra trips to make it possible for her to pick up the document.

When Sue confronted John with forgetting, he felt extremely guilty. Instead of maintaining those unproductive thoughts, he made up for his lack of consideration by running one of her errands for her.

When he took action and did something about his guilty feelings, there was no reason for him to feel guilty and as a result the feeling dissipated.

In his article, "Guilt Feelings as an Excuse" in <u>Psychodynamics, Psychotherapy and Counseling</u>: Collected papers: Alfred Adler Institute, 1967; Rudolf Dreikurs wrote:

*"Guilt feelings appear only if one is unwilling to amend and is still trying to maintain the assumption of his good intentions. As soon as sincere efforts are made to atone or amend, guilt feelings disappear."*

## WORRY example:

Ann invested a large sum of money in the stock market. In the last several days, her investment had been dropping. Ann couldn't get to sleep because she was worrying about what to do. Even though she spent many hours thinking, she still didn't have a decision about what action she was going to take.

Notice how Ann has immobilized herself. She can't sleep and she isn't productive at work. While she's worrying, she can't take action. What she needs to do is to find out what her alternatives are. Perhaps she feels that researching alternatives will result in embarrassment or she may fear that she will make the wrong decision. As a result, she replaces action with worry. The irony is that she would be better off if she would make **any** decision, act on it and get on with her life.

## JEALOUSY For the purpose of control:

Andrea and Matt went to a party. After the party, Matt started to accuse Andrea of dancing too close with a neighbor. Andrea made the necessary explanations to calm him down but the residue feeling was that, in the future, she would do anything she could to minimize Matt's jealousy of the neighbor.

Matt controlled Andrea's behavior by feeling jealous. He was comparing himself with the neighbor and dealt with his own lack of self-confidence by getting Andrea to feel as she had better "watch her step" around the neighbor.

## JEALOUSY For the purpose of getting attention:

"You spent more time talking to Joan than you did me," pouted Marilyn. "You think she's more interesting than me."

"Now, you know that's not true. I love you and I think you're the most interesting person I've met," pleaded Allan.

"Well, how come you spent so much time with her then?" Marilyn retaliated.

This discussion continued for another ten minute without producing a solution. Marilyn did accomplish one thing. She managed to get Allan's undivided attention.

### JEALOUSY For the purpose of getting even:

Tom said he was going to be *"out with the boys"* and he would be back at one. Tom ambled home at three and was very drunk. Amy was extremely hurt by his lack of consideration and wanted to strike back. She knew one of his touchy subjects was his old girl friend so she lashed out, *"What's the matter? aren't I good enough for you? I suppose not. You probably went and messed around with Linda. She's just your type. You two deserve each other!"*

Notice how Amy is saying hurtful things to Tom. Often, when we feel powerless to get what we want, we give up our original desires and settle for revenge. Amy is underestimating her ability to win Tom's affection. She is comparing herself to Linda. She feels powerless and sees no way of getting what she wants. She believes that her only alternative is to hurt Tom the way she feels hurt.

Jealousy is the ideal disguise for revenge because it makes it appear that we are only reacting to the pain we are feeling. Jealousy is a way to say, *"I really love you even though I am hurting you."* Jealousy is often erroneously defined as the natural response to fear of the loss of a loved one. This is not true. If Amy was afraid that she was going to lose Tom, the logical response would be to do things to win him over, not to be hostile to him!

### JEALOUSY For the purpose of hiding your shortcomings:

Patti was out of town on business. While she was away she had an affair. When she returned home she questioned her husband about why she was unable to reach him by phone the night before. She accused him of going out with another woman. Her husband was so busy defending himself that it never occurred to him that she might be having an affair.

Patti's jealousy served the purpose of distracting her husband from seeing her shortcomings.

**DREAMS example:**
See "THE MYSTERY OF DREAMS" later in this chapter.

**HOSTILE FEELINGS example:**
One day we were driving home from a ski trip and I realized that I was entertaining hostile feelings toward our attorney.

Several weeks earlier, I had made arrangements for Mrs. Smith, who lived in another state, to send me a check for $100 to pay for my attorney's travel expenses so that he could take her deposition. A short time after making the arrangements with Mrs. Smith, I was in my attorney's office. He said, *"I need a check from you for $100 so I can go take Mrs. Smith's deposition."* I told him that I had not yet received the check from Mrs. Smith. He said, *"I talked to her on the phone. She will give me the check when I get there, but I need the $100 from you now."* Reluctantly I gave him $100. When he returned from taking her deposition he said, *"By the way, Mrs. Smith said she would mail you the check."*

Driving along I was feeling very hostile because I felt my attorney had disrupted the arrangements I had made. I was concerned that I would never get the $100 check from Mrs. Smith. Realizing that I had hostile feelings, I asked myself what the situation was demanding of me. I came to the conclusion that I was avoiding the task of calling Mrs. Smith to ask for my money. Instead of placing the call, which is what I should have done, I was stirring up hostile feelings about what my attorney should not have done.

What was there in my life style (the convictions that I formulated as a child) that was making me avoid asking for my money? A quick review of some of my early recollections led me to the answer.

When I was a child my uncle would visit us and would always give me a dollar bill. One night I had to go to bed before he had arrived. As my father was tucking me into bed I said, *"When my uncle gets here be sure to get my dollar bill for me."* My father was very unhappy with me and expressed his disapproval. He told me that it was bad to ask for a gift.

Evidently I misinterpreted this to mean that I should never ask for money under any circumstances. Being aware of hostile feelings helped me to identify the prejudice I had about asking for my money. I was surprised to recognize how closely my early recollection fit my predicament with my attorney. I was even more surprised when I realized that the reason that I was hiring the attorney in the first place was that I was suing a man for whom I had worked without getting paid. It was another example of how I had allowed myself to get into trouble by not asking for my money.

Once I recognized this mistake in my life style, I immediately decided that I wanted to get over this subconscious fear. Today I am the person in our office who is best at calling past due accounts and getting them to pay.

**ANGER example:**
Alex had asked Sandra not to play the piano while he was on the phone. An important client called and Sandra continued to play. After the phone conversation, Alex stomped over to the piano, slammed down the cover to the piano keys and hollered, *"Why can't you ever do what I ask?!"* His wife got defensive and said that she had not realized that he was on the phone. Alex stomped into his study and slammed the door.

Alex successfully intimidated Sandra. However, his rude behavior allowed Sandra to think about how obnoxious Alex was instead of thinking about how she was in the wrong. His intimidation didn't persuade her to respect his wishes. However, Alex did receive a benefit. He had felt unsuccessful with his business conversation. Intimidating Sandra allowed him to feel powerful.

You might be able to intimidate someone to do or not to do something. However, this is a small consolation prize for what you really want - closeness. A person can't be close to you if they are afraid of you.

**SELF-ANGER for the purpose of making yourself feel as if you are doing something:**
Fred had been laid off work five weeks ago. One morning he said to his wife, *"I'm so angry at myself! I still haven't found a job. What's wrong with me anyway?"* His wife took up his defense saying, *"It's OK honey, you've been trying."* He spent the rest of that day repairing the toaster.

Fred's self anger allowed him to feel as if he had done something about his problem. He used this feeling to justify his decision to postpone his job search. If he had not been so discouraged about his ability to get a job, he might have used this same self anger to explore why he was being unsuccessful.

**SELF-ANGER for the purpose of influencing others to not make demands on you:**
Phil and Roger were playing tennis with two other friends. Roger was hitting some lousy shots. Each time he made a bad shot, he would swear at himself or hit his racket on the net. It was as if he was saying to his teammate, *"See how angry I am at myself? See how hard I'm trying?"* As a result, Phil didn't dare complain about Roger's bad shots.

This tactic makes it hard for the other party to make demands on you to perform better because you are already being so hard on yourself.

51

**SELF-ANGER for the purpose of self-motivation:**
Marge had allowed her husband to take advantage of her. He had called and said that he was bringing his boss home for dinner. She had agreed, although she really didn't want to cook at home. She had to give up her plans for the day in order to go food shopping, clean house and prepare the meal.

While shopping she felt very angry at herself. She used her self anger to motivate herself to look at what she had done wrong to cause herself this problem. She concluded that she should have told her husband that she would prefer to take his boss out to dinner. As soon as she realized what she could have done to avoid the problem her anger subsided.

Marge was feeling angry at herself because this seemed to be a pattern in her life, not only with her husband but also with friends. She often agreed when she didn't want to. The more angry she got, the more determined she was not to let it happen again.


**TEMPER example:**
See "FINDING YOUR TEMPER" later in this chapter.


**BOREDOM for the purpose of asking someone else to make your life interesting:**
Eight-year-old Scott whined to his mother, *"I'm bored."* His mom responded, *"Why don't you play with your Legos?"* *"That's no fun,"* replied Scott. Mom went on making suggestions until Scott was finally satisfied.

Scott was learning that someone else is responsible for making his life interesting. When he gets older he may be attracted to activities that promise excitement without much effort on his part, such as watching TV or smoking pot. He may tend to miss out on the enjoyment of being an active participator.

**BOREDOM for the purpose of rebelling against life's demands:**

Sam felt bored with his job. He said that he didn't think that being a production manager was what he really wanted to do for a living. However, he had no idea as to what he did want to do.

After examining the situation, we discovered that his supervisor was not holding Sam responsible. His supervisor seemed to be acting on the theory of, *"If I just allow Sam to do whatever he wants and never hold him accountable, then maybe he will do his best for me."* For example:

Sam and his supervisor would set weekly production goals. If Sam didn't meet his goals, his supervisor would not say anything, nor would he give Sam any suggestions as to what he could do to accomplish the goals. The supervisor would just pick up the slack for Sam. Without being accountable or making a commitment it was impossible for Sam to feel a sense of satisfaction from his work.

One of the ways to achieve satisfaction in life is to make commitments and hold ourselves accountable. When we don't hold ourselves accountable we allow ourselves to slide through life - only doing what we can *"get by with."* That attitude causes us to lose respect for ourselves and for the situation we are in. We then can't experience the joy of victory or the agony of defeat.

We asked Sam to make a commitment to his employer. We said to him, *"Would you be willing to make a commitment to increase the production of your department by 10% by the end of next month?"*

Sam became very uncomfortable. He said he could make that commitment; however, he didn't want to because he had lost interest in the work he was doing.

We inquired into Sam's early experiences in order to discover why he felt it necessary to avoid commitment.

We asked him, *"What was the first time you remember feeling pain or disappointment?"* He shared this story:

> *"I was in kindergarten and we moved. I had to go to a new school. I didn't know anything or anybody. I was just wandering around. No one offered to help, nor did I ask for help. I felt scared and alienated."*

It appeared that the purpose of Sam's boredom was to avoid getting into a position where he would end up needing help and be unable to get it. His boredom was his way to protect himself from feeling scared and alienated. It was a covert rebellion against life's demands. Life was demanding that he trust his own judgment or get the help he needed. However, he felt:

> *"If I get in a situation where I have to commit myself, I can't trust others to help me and I can't trust myself to ask for the help I need. It would be best for me to avoid the whole situation by being bored."*

Had Sam felt that he could get the help he needed, he would not have needed his boredom. When he started participating at 100% the job became interesting!

**LOVE example:**
See Chapter 6 "THE OTHER SEX"

**DEPRESSION example:**
When Brenda was a child her mother felt very responsible for Brenda's happiness. Brenda concluded that all she needed to do was to look sad. Then someone else would come to the rescue and solve the problem. Now, as an adult, she assumes a sad depressed posture whenever things don't go her way.

Depression is like having a silent temper tantrum. It is a way to urge someone else to give you what you want.

## OVERCOMING DISCOURAGEMENT

Many of us have been taught that depression is a negative emotion — that you shouldn't feel discouraged. However, we can learn about ourselves by asking our selves, *"Why am I depressing myself?"* (When we say we *"are depressed"* instead of saying we are *"depressing ourselves"* we are shunning responsibility for our moods.)

Sometimes situations arise where we feel unprepared to meet the demands that are placed upon us. As a result we evoke feelings of hopelessness so that we can justify, to ourselves and others, our choice to give up. For example:

Phil and Sue got divorced. Phil was feeling apprehensive about his abilities to form a relationship with someone else. One of the ways he tried to postpone the task of making a choice was by getting depressed. Phil lacked the courage to choose.

He saw choosing another partner as a risky proposition. His depression justified his hesitation.

## REASONS FOR DEPRESSION

Here are some reasons why we might choose discouragement instead of choosing to be more courageous:

A situation occurs -we feel inadequate- we decide to give up in order to:

**1. GET SYMPATHY** At least sympathy alleviates some of the inadequacy we feel. Sometimes we misinterpret getting sympathy as a way of being loved or achieving intimacy. It may feel good to have someone feel sorry for us. But we underestimate the price we pay to achieve sympathy. In order to get others to feel sorry for us, we have to remain in a one-down position. This erodes our self-confidence and makes us feel like we don't have control over our lives. Another disadvantage is that, people may be willing to give you sympathy for awhile, but it becomes wearing. Most people enjoy being around people who take control of their lives.

**2. GET HELP** In the past others have helped us solve our problems whenever we looked sad.

**3. AVOID DEMANDS** If we're depressed we can avoid having to live up to the demands that are placed upon us by life or by others.

**4. GET OTHERS TO CHANGE** If we are miserable then perhaps the other person will see how miserable we are and will change their ways. It is a way of saying *"Look what you have done to me!"* in hopes that this will somehow influence the other person. (Occasionally we also do this to hurt the other person.)

**5. MOTIVATE OURSELVES.** If we make ourselves miserable, we will get sick and tired of being sick and tired. This feeling that we create helps us motivate ourselves to do something about the problem.

## ANGER DISGUISED AS DEPRESSION

Many of us were not taught how to express anger appropriately. In fact, some of us were taught that it is not appropriate to be angry at all. You may want to explore this further by answering the following questions:

How did your mother express anger?

How did your father express anger?

How did the sibling the most different from you express anger?

How did you as a child express anger?

What results did each person get when they expressed their anger?

What were the family values toward expressing anger?

How do you express anger as an adult?

For example: John's mother never really expressed her anger openly. However, you knew she was angry because she gave the family the silent treatment. This made them feel so guilty for how miserable they made her feel that they would go out of their way to make it up to her.

John's father expressed his anger by showing his family how disgusted he was with them. Usually, this made John feel like doing the opposite of what his father wanted.

The sibling most different from him, showed his anger by having open temper tantrums. John's parents would punish his brother for the tantrums. John decided that he didn't want to get punished for throwing temper tantrums. So he decided to model his mother's display of anger and looked sad when he was angry.

John has a tendency to give his wife and family the *"silent treatment"* when he is angry with them.

In the above example, John learned to make himself miserable when he was angry at someone else.

## DISCOURAGING YOURSELF
The following is a list of ways we discourage ourselves and some suggestions of how to encourage yourself. Of course, you first need to decide not to be discouraged. If you haven't made that decision then this list won't help.

## 1. Making excuses:
Realize that making mistakes is a part of being human. There is no need to justify or explain your behavior. Doing so puts you in a one-down position which only adds to your discouragement.

## 2. Blaming others:

Recognize that blaming never accomplishes anything. It only allows you to have an escape from having to take responsibility for what happens in your life. You can't improve or learn about yourself while you're concentrating on what others have done wrong. Ask yourself, "In what way did I not protect myself?"

## 3. Imagining the worst:

Ask yourself what is the worst that could happen and develop a plan to handle it.

## 4. Running a conflict over and over in your mind:

Imagine the conflict ending just the way you would like it to end. Then concentrate on what you would do next if it actually ended that way. This prevents you from using worry to avoid getting on with your life.

## 5. Striving for perfection:

Ask yourself, *"What is one small improvement that I can make?"*

## 6. Stressing the importance of the final product:

Enjoy the process. Ask yourself, *"Am I having fun right now?"*

## 7. Overwhelm yourself with long lists:

Make a short achievable list.

## 8. Being critical of self and others:

See yourself and others as human and look for the humor of the situation. Do something to encourage yourself or others. Ask yourself, *"What's going on in my life right now that is making me feel so inadequate that I find it necessary to prove that I am better than others?"*

## 9. Expecting others to know what you want:

Tell others what you want. Stop testing them to see if they love you .

## 10. Getting defeated by failure or criticism:

Ask yourself, *"What can I learn from this failure or criticism?"*

## 11. Comparing:

Recognize that whenever you are comparing you are trying to fight the idea that someone else may be better than you. There is always someone better than you. And you are often better than others. So what?

## 12. Holding grudges:

Ask yourself why you are afraid to discuss your complaint with the other person.

## 13. Being resentful:

Arrange to get more of what YOU want.

## 14. Procrastinating:

Picture what you would do if you went ahead and then failed. Make a plan for how you would recover.

## 15. Doing too much of one activity; i.e.., working, sleeping, reading, watching TV, eating:

Take more risks. Develop more of an appetite for life by trying new activities.

**16. Hoping that when such and such happens, then you'll be happy:**

Make arrangements to enjoy life now. Don't "wait" for it.

**17. Not knowing what you want:**

Experiment to find what you want. Try things for the purpose of discovering what you DON'T want.

You may find that you resist following some of these suggestions by simply "understanding" them. Did you find yourself saying, *"I know that."* If so, then reread the list and decide which of the suggestions you will use. Don't just "understand", do it!

If you try some of these techniques and your discouragement still persists, you may want to see a counselor to get further suggestions.

**FINDING YOUR TEMPER**

A man driving his car down the street suddenly and intentionally steers right up on the sidewalk and runs over several pedestrians.

If the police catch this chap, they lock him up for murder.

However, a man is driving his car down the street. As he turns the corner the door flies open and he falls out. His car continues to swerve down the street. It goes up on the sidewalk and runs over several pedestrians.

In this case, we are not as harsh on the offender because he was not in control of the car when it infringed on the rights of the pedestrians.

How does this relate to temper? Let us ask, *"When you lose your temper, where do you find it afterwards? Does it roll under the sofa? "I'm sorry, I didn't mean to yell at you. I lost my temper."* What you are really saying with this statement is, *"I want to intimidate you and scare you to my way of thinking, but please don't blame me - my driver fell out!"*

You may claim that you can't help losing your temper. You may say, *"What am I supposed to do with all that pent up anger?"* If you had a bad taste in your mouth you would spit it out. But, you wouldn't spit it in someone's face! Losing your temper is not done to relieve pressure - it is done to intimidate others.

Losing your temper is a way of not feeling responsible. If you have often felt helpless because you have lost your temper, we would suggest that you do the following exercise.

Pretend you are an actor or actress and your part in the movie is to be an irate boss. Your employee was late. You are very very angry. You are screaming at him and threatening to fire him if he is ever late again.

Go ahead. Act out the part. Remember that you are playing the part of a real tyrant. Scream, pound your fist on the desk, jump up and down and get red in the face. If you want to get over your temper, put the book down and do this exercise before reading the next page. Do it now.

If you completed the assignment you have just shown yourself that you can control your temper. If you gave it a try but didn't really act angry, then you are probably trying to convince yourself that you do not have control of your anger. You are most likely trying to reserve the right to say, *"Don't blame me, I lost my temper."*

## THE MYSTERY OF DREAMS

What are our dreams? Are they messages from the great beyond? Are they symbols of guidance from a source of greater intelligence? I can remember one occasion when I was a teenager and wanted to find out what others thought about dreams. I had decided to make a telephone survey. I was going to phone 100 people and inquire as to their beliefs about dreams.

I dialed the first number and a man answered. I told him my name and said that I was taking a survey on what people believed about dreams and said, *"What do you think dreams are?"* He hung up! So did the next five people that I called. That was the end of my survey, but not the end of my curiosity. Why did they all hang up? Maybe it was my fault. Perhaps I didn't sound serious enough and caused them to think it was a prank call. Perhaps they didn't know how to answer the question, *"What do you think dreams are?"*

An even more interesting possibility is that perhaps they didn't want to understand dreams better. Maybe they felt that if they were forced to explore their opinions about the purpose of dreaming, then dreaming would lose its usefulness.

My subsequent study of dreams has led me to believe this latter reason has the best possibility of being accurate. Through use with many of our clients, we have come to believe that Alfred Adler's theory of dreams is the most accurate and the most useful.

## THE FACTORY OF EMOTIONS

Adler considered dreams as the *"factory of emotions and feelings."* He did not see dreams as being the product of past trauma or previous experiences. We have already survived all of our previous experiences! We aren't concerned about yesterday. It's today and tomorrow that challenge us. We need to consider how our dreams are being used to help us prepare for the future.

## YOUR UNRECOGNIZED CREATIVITY

You create the story, not only choose but also create and design the cast, design and construct the set, direct the play and occasionally even play one or more of the roles. And even more amazing, you create and perform several of these masterpieces every night of the year. And it is a rare occasion when you repeat a performance. Almost every play has a totally unique plot!

Are you giving yourself credit for the creative ability you display in your dreams? Let's explore how we use all of these creative masterpieces.

When asleep, we are not limited by the demands of reality. We can construct whatever situations fit our purposes.

In our waking life, we are faced with having to decide how to deal with an upcoming challenge. The logic of common sense may conflict with what we want to do in order to stay within the limitations of our life style. Reality may be limiting our options or may be making it difficult for us to justify the action we plan to take.

## MY HEART ISN'T IN IT

While asleep we create an experience, and this experience leaves us with certain feelings. The following day we can justify our actions, based upon our feelings.

Example: Tony said, *"I really want it to work out with my wife Julie but I'm so much in love with Laura that I'm afraid if I stay with Julie I won't be able to make her happy. I'm really trying but it seems as if my heart just really isn't in it. I can't stop thinking of Laura."*

Notice how Tony is saying that he has good intentions about keeping his commitment to his wife. However, because of his feelings (for which he claims no responsibility) he would be doing his wife a favor by breaking his commitment to her. If it wasn't for those evil feelings that are to blame for everything, he would be a really good guy.

We asked Tony to tell us about one of his recent dreams.

*"I dreamt that I was a king. There was a war going on and everyone was scared. They were running in all directions screaming, 'What shall we do?' I told them to go to the tower and shoot arrows. I went to the tower but all the invading soldiers had run away."*

How was this dream related to Tony's decision to leave his wife? How was it helping him create his uncontrollable feelings of love for Laura?

Tony's wife, Julie was an extremely independent woman. She was self-employed and prided herself in not needing anyone's help. Laura was considerably younger than Tony, just beginning her career. Tony's attraction to her was in the way she *"always looks up to me for advice."*

The dream helped Tony feel, *"I'll be a successful king if I can get into a situation where others are desperate for my advice."* He created his dream to help him feel that it is to his advantage to be with dependent people, and if he takes on that role, even the enemy (Julie) won't get hurt - she'll just run away. Notice how this compares to Tony's feelings of, *"If I don't go with Laura , Julie will get hurt."*

We asked Tony if he had any idea why he had this dream. He told us that he thought it was because the night before he was watching a movie on TV about a castle.

He thought that the movie was responsible for the dream. When in actuality, he only used components from the movie to construct the scenario that would help him develop the feelings he desired. He had no intentions of keeping the commitment to his wife. The feelings he created were to help him maintain a clear conscience while breaking his commitment.

## THE PURPOSE OF OUR DREAMS

Once we know the purpose of our dreams we can use them to gain self insight and to minimize the mischief that we may otherwise create.

Although it is often difficult to recognize the purpose of our own dreams and may require the help of a professional counselor, you can use a formula to gain some self insight. It requires the courage to be imperfect and a little practice. It can be a very effective self-therapy tool. Here is the five step process:

## 5 STEPS TO INTERPRET YOUR OWN DREAMS

Step 1. Upon waking, write down your dream and the residue feelings.

Step 2. Make a list of several of the upcoming tests or challenges which are confronting you.

Step 3. Look for how the feelings created in the dream may be used to perform mischief as related to one of the upcoming challenges.

Step 4. Look for a courageous way that the feelings created in the dream could be used in conjunction with the upcoming challenges.

Step 5. Say to yourself in a real spirit of adventure, *"It will be interesting to see if I will choose to do the mischief or if I will do the courageous thing."*

Example: John used the five step approach with the following dream:

Step 1. The dream:
*"I was swimming under water and I could see all the pebbles on the bottom of the lake. Everything was crystal*

*clear. I could stay under water as long as I liked, even though I was not using any kind of breathing apparatus."*

The feeling:
*"I felt very free and confident."*

Step 2.  List of upcoming challenges:
1.  Should I buy a new car?
2.  I have to go to a party Saturday night.
3.  I need to decide which bills to pay.
4.  I'm planning on building shelves in the garage.
5.  My boss wants a written report by Wednesday.

Step 3.  If I were up to mischief:
*"Perhaps I wanted to make myself feel over-confident, as if I were super human and could do anything. Why would I want to feel that way? Perhaps it relates to my desire to buy a new car. I really don't think I can afford it but I really want a new car. Maybe if I feel superhuman, I can justify buying the car based upon the feeling that I can increase my income later. Perhaps feeling that I can see everything perfectly clear will allow me to avoid a close examination of my personal finances. That way I can just go and get what I want even though it may cause me to be unfair to my creditors later."*

Step 4.  If I intend to do the courageous thing:
*"Maybe I created that feeling of 'It feels good to see things perfectly clear' so that I take the time to thoroughly investigate my financial situation and all the other facts about the purchase. Then I can make a more appropriate decision."*

Step 5 *"It will be interesting to see what I decide to do."*


**WHY IT WORKS**

Even though, because of your own bias, it may be difficult for you to pinpoint the exact purpose for the dream, you can still improve your chances of avoiding mischief; i.e..,

John's dream may have really pertained to the challenge of going to a party or the demands his boss was placing on him. However, due to using the above process he will make a better decision about buying the new car.

After admitting to himself that he may be in the process of ignoring the financial facts (step 3) and then considering a more social alternative (step 4) it is not likely that he will make an inconsiderate purchase.

Dreikurs referred to the process of disclosing an individual's possible mischief as *"spitting in your soup."* It doesn't make it impossible to eat the soup, but somehow it is no longer quite so appetizing.

We suggest that at the same time you *"spit in your bowl of mischief soup,"* you also provide yourself with an alternative bowl of *"courageous soup."* With these two choices available it becomes much easier to move in a direction which will be your greatest benefit, thus avoiding costly *"expedient"* decisions.

## THE PROFESSOR'S DREAM

A college professor shared with us how he used the five steps to interpret one of his dreams.

Step 1. The dream:
*"I got to the classroom on time. All the students were there, but something was missing. The school hadn't provided what was necessary, so I left and went somewhere that I wanted to be, but I ended up getting involved in having a good time."*

*"I was watching the clock. The class was supposed to start at 8:30 and it was now 11:00. I was thinking, 'Should I even go back and try to salvage the day?' I wondered if any people were still waiting there. By the time I figured out how to solve the problem myself, as opposed to letting the school solve it, it was 11:30. I went back , but only a*

*couple of students were still waiting. All the ones who left were probably angry. I thought it was OK with the ones who stayed because if they waited this long they must be thinking as I do and I'll be able to win them over."*

The feeling:
*"Oh no!! It's too late. Something heavy is coming up. In some way energized and some way inadequate. I felt flexibility still being able to make it go even if it was a mess."*

Step #2. List of upcoming challenges:
1. Should I have children.
2. I need to do my income tax report.
3. My wife's student loan may be cut.
4. I need to give a lecture.

Step #3. If I were up to mischief:
*"Perhaps I am doubting my ability to do a great job on the lecture. Maybe I created the dream to help me feel that the others won't do their part. Maybe I'll start putting excessive demands on others that they can't possibly fulfill. Then if I do a lousy job on the lecture it will be the school's fault, not mine."*

Step #4. If I intend to do the courageous thing:
*"Perhaps I created this dream to keep me from being too dependent upon others. Maybe I'll use those feelings to motivate myself to accept more responsibility myself."*

Step #5. *"It will be interesting to see what I decide to do."*

Don't overlook the importance of step five. Life is challenging, and to face life courageously we need to avoid condemning ourselves or our own mischief. This method won't be effective if you say to yourself, *"Oh no! I better not do the mischief."* What is needed is a courageous adventuresome spirit where you will feel OK about yourself even if you do choose to do the mischief. That's what is meant by the *"courage to be imperfect."*

# *Chapter Three*

tm

# OUR OPINIONS OF OURSELVES

### Opinions

What makes people the way they are? What is personality, and how is it formed? Consider the following two points:

1.  Personality is the set of opinions we have formed about ourselves, life and others.

2.  Our opinions were formulated from decisions we made. Those decisions were based upon the way we interpreted our early situations.

When we view personality as a collection of factors which are shaped by the conclusions and meanings that the child assigns, we discover a greater freedom to change any human characteristic we find limiting. Opinions can always be changed.

Let's look closer at personality.

## THE SPACE SHIP

Look around the room and find a closed door. Walk out that door, then come back in. How did you walk out? Our guess is that you walked right out. No hesitation. No checking it out first. You just confidently walked out.

Now walk out the same door again, only this time change the scenery. Pretend you are in a space ship. The ship has just landed on a strange planet in a distant and unknown galaxy. No one has ever been here before. You have no idea if the air outside is breathable, or if there are hostile creatures standing outside waiting to attack the first person to walk out. Under these circumstances, how would you walk out the door?

Would you hesitate, or refuse to go out? Would you sniff around the door as you cracked it open, and then peek outside before cautiously proceeding?

Why weren't you cautious in the first instance? You are probably thinking, *"Because the first time I knew what to expect."* Did you really know what to expect, or did you only **ACT AS IF** you knew what to expect?

Let's look at the situation objectively. The first time you walked out the door, is it not possible that the air outside may have been poisoned as a result of a chemical truck accident? Is it not possible that a desperate person may have been outside waiting to attack the first person to walk out? Although these events are possible, the odds are not in favor of them occurring. We therefore assume a bias that it is safe to walk freely out the door. The adoption of such biases is crucial to help us deal with the uncertainties of life. We all adopt beliefs in order to move "safely" through life. Without them, we would be unable to participate in life.

With this in mind let us redefine **personality** as:

**an individual's collection of biases (beliefs or decisions) about life, himself and others, and his perception of what he needs to do in order to belong, feel important, stay safe, and participate in life.**

Our personality is our unique, personal collection of beliefs about life which we use to help us choose our actions. If we feel it is safe or if we think it is to our advantage, we will walk through an unknown doorway without hesitation. If we feel it is unsafe or to our disadvantage, we will hesitate or refuse. But the decision is based upon our expectations, not on certainty.

We all need to have a personality. Without it we would be constantly intimidated into inaction because we could not ascertain what would happen in the next moment.

## MISINTERPRETATIONS

We form our expectations or generalizations about life in childhood, based upon our interpretations of early experiences. We size up our predicament and create a series of perceptions, or a **"life style"** which we use in order to participate and establish a feeling of belonging.

As we grow older, our "life style" provides us with a notion as to:

What to expect from life.
What to expect from others.
What to expect from our own abilities.
What is our best chance to have a place and belong.

These values are often cherished into adulthood. The inaccuracies of these perceptions are the source of many adult conflicts.

Since these values are formed during our childhood at a time when we are in a position of disadvantage, there is a substantial likelihood for misinterpretation. Some of the major influences which we may have misinterpreted as a child are:

**Birth order**
**Age differences**
**Sex**
**Handicaps or health problems**
**Social setting**
**Tragedies in the family**
**Sibling competition**
**Family values**
**Parental response**

We will explore some of the possible ways that an individual may have interpreted each of these influencing factors and make some generalizations. Remember however, that these are only generalizations. To get a more specific understanding of yourself answer the questions that follow each section.

**BIRTH ORDER:**

**FIRST-BORN**

First-borns tend to be more conservative. Probably because parents tend to be more conservative in the parenting approaches when dealing with their first child. Usually, by the time the second or third child arrives the parents' methods are more relaxed.

First-borns are frequently more conscious of responsibility and meeting the expectations of others. This excessive emphasis on being responsible is often established because they often concluded, *"I can be special by flaunting* (to the other siblings) *that I know what Mom or Dad wants."* i.e.., *"Mom said that you shouldn't do that. You are really going to get in trouble if you don't stop."* They tend to be

72

achievement-oriented due to parents' expectations of the first born. *"Now Sue, you're the oldest. You should know better than that."* Frequently, this drive to be competent is more of a burden or an obligation than something that is enjoyable. This sense of obligation often results in a feeling of resentment.

They tend to be good leaders because they have spent most of their childhood guiding or taking care of younger siblings. The following are comments frequently expressed by first-borns:

*"I tend to be too responsible for other people."*

*"I work more than I should."*

*"Others expect a lot from me."*

*"I get tired of always having to be the strongest, or having to take care of everyone."*

## MIDDLE CHILDREN

Middle children of a smaller family have different characteristics than middle children in a larger family. The middle child of three tends to be either more openly rebellious or more withdrawn than the other two children. They are often the most different in the family. For example, the oldest and youngest may get good grades. The middle may get poor grades but become involved in sports, music, or exhibit the misbehavior in the family.

Middle children in a larger family tend to go to less extremes to become different. Their sense of trying to find an identity often persists into adulthood. As a result of having to deal with so many people, they tend to be more flexible and often more sociable. However, they often underestimate their ability to get what they want.

Comments frequently expressed by middle children:

*"I had a hard time finding a place for myself in my family. I noticed that I feel the same way when I'm with a group of friends."*

*"I had the opportunity to observe what my brother and sisters did to achieve or get into trouble. So it was easy for me to figure out what would work. In adult life, I am a keen observer and easily find the path of least resistance."*

*"I was the only girl in the middle of two boys and got stuck with more than my share of the housework. I still feel taken advantage of in that area of my life."*

## YOUNGEST CHILDREN

Youngest tend to be more carefree. They have never been dethroned by another baby. Often, less is expected of this child. This could free up the youngest to excel and sometimes over-compensate for being the youngest or it could undermine the youngest's self-confidence. In the latter case, the youngest may expect a certain amount of pampering or specialness as an adult, which could lead to a disturbance in relationships. They sometimes spend a lifetime trying to prove that they really are important.

Here are comments expressed by youngest children:

*"Sometimes, I feel others don't take me seriously."*

*"I was the clown of my family. As an adult, I enjoy being funny with my friends."*

*"A lot of things were done for me as a child. I often doubt my ability to handle situations."*

## ONLY CHILDREN

Only children also have a sense of high achievement. Probably because there are no other children to fulfill the parents' expectations. They had the undivided attention of both Mother and Father. As a result, they are often more self-confident in one-on-one situations.

Frequently, they tend to be more adept at getting along with older or younger people than they do with people of the same age since they had no siblings to learn how to get along with. Occasionally they go through life on tip toes trying to appear bigger than they feel.

Comments made by only children:

*"I never had to share my possessions as a child. Sometimes I have a hard time sharing things now."*

*"I had to entertain myself as a child. I find that I enjoy being alone more than most people."*

There are always exceptions to these patterns. It is important that you look at each individual situation. The characteristics developed by birth order positioning are only opinions that a person develops. As a result, they are not static, and different patterns that would be more useful to that person can always be relearned.

## QUESTIONS

What birth order position were you? How did you feel in that position? Are there any similarities between how you felt in that position and how you feel now? In what way were you different than your sisters and brothers?

## AGE DIFFERENCES

Age differences in the family can also affect the way a person views life. For example, the person who has a sibling six years older than her may develop characteristics more similar to that of an only child rather than a youngest.

In the following example, because of the large age gap between Jim and Sara, Sara developed characteristics that were more typical of an oldest child. This was because she was the oldest child of a second set of children. She did not develop middle child characteristics. Consider this age grouping:

Fred    age 35
Jim     age 34
Sara    age 24
Julie   age 23
Mike    age 20

Also, there was only eighteen months difference between Fred and Jim. This made it possible for Jim to overtake his older brother. Jim became more outgoing and excelled in sports whereas Fred became discouraged and was known in high school as the *"weakling"*. Had there been a four year age difference between Fred and Jim, it would have been almost impossible for Jim to become more physical than his older brother. In that case Fred may have been the one to choose to develop his athletic skills.

## QUESTION

How did the age difference between you and your brothers or sisters influence the decisions you made about how to find a place in your family?

## SEX

The attitude of the parents as to what they expect from children of each sex can determine how that child feels about himself and what he expects from himself. For example:

In the Johnson family, there is a boy eight and a girl six. When the boy gets hurt and starts to cry, the parent responds by saying, *"Now stop crying and be a big boy!"* Whereas, when the girl gets hurts and cries, she is comforted.

The son is being trained to become callused and to influence people with his strength. The girl is being trained to influence people by using her helplessness and dependence.

In a family with three children of the same sex, there tends to be more competition than in a family where there is a girl between two boys, or a boy between girls. Probably because the different sex has a special place just because they are of the other sex. It also breaks up the years between the similar sexes. We often find that the more years between the siblings, the less competition.


## QUESTIONS

Were boys and girls treated differently in your family? How did you feel about it? How does it relate to how you feel about sex now?

## SIBLING COMPETITION

By sibling competition we do not necessarily mean outward aggression shown by one sibling against the other. Competition as Adler defined it, is the process whereby one child gives up in an area in which his sibling succeeds. He does this in order to avoid comparison- in other words it is a fear of competition. A fear of not being able to measure up in that area.

One child might excel in music and the other sibling might excel in sports. Often the child who doesn't do well in the area of his sibling's expertise feels that he does not have talent in that area. In reality, he too could achieve. He has only made a decision not to practice and develop those skills. Here is an example of sibling competition:

Bill, co-author of this book, plays the drums. He has excellent rhythm and at one point had his own band. However, he did not enjoy dancing, he says he feels awkward. I could never understand why a person with such good rhythm should lack confidence on the dance floor. One day when we were looking through pictures in his family album, I saw a photo of his older sister in a gorgeous fur lined dance costume. When I asked Bill to tell me about the picture, he explained that his sister got special attention for being a dancer. After our discussion, Bill recognized that it's not that he's a clumsy dancer, but that he had given up practicing as a result of the competition. He decided to start practicing and he now enjoys dancing.

## QUESTIONS

Have you given up on any activity because a sibling succeeded in that area? Would you like to develop those skills?

## HANDICAPS AND HEALTH PROBLEMS

If a member of the family has a handicap or health problem, it can not only affect the way the person with the difficulty views life, it can also affect the way others in the family view life. For example:

Fred had a father who had a heart condition. Members of the family were expected not to express anger openly or make demands because that might upset their father. As a result, Fred learned to express his displeasure from a posture of resentment. He resigned himself to give up negotiating with others. He would frequently put up with things and feel resentful, but would never get angry.

Often, if one child is ill or needs additional care, it changes the positioning in the family. For example, if the oldest is sickly, the second child often develops characteristics similar to that of a first-born. Or if the second to the last is sickly, he or she often takes the place of the youngest.

## QUESTIONS

Was there anyone who was frequently sick in your family? How did it effect the decisions you made as a child as to what you needed to do in order to be important?

## SOCIAL SETTING

The values of the community in which a person lives help mold the person's opinion of life. Not too many years ago, if a woman wanted to work out of the home she was frowned upon. Therefore few women developed skills for occupations outside the home. To establish these community values, girls were encouraged to play with dolls while boys were frequently asked, *"What will you be when you grow up?"*

In our current society it is generally becoming more acceptable for women to work outside the home. This will. create many new alternatives for both men and women. Our attitudes about children's toys and games are changing to reflect these new social values. For more information on the effects of our current social situation see Chapter 4.

## QUESTIONS

What were the values of the community you lived in? Did you accept the values or did you fight them? Compare your list of values to the list at the beginning of Chapter 4. Which column fits the way you were raised?

## TRAGEDIES IN THE FAMILY

Frequently when a tragedy such as death or a serious injury occurs, children in the family often assume more responsibility for what happens than is necessary. When they become an adult they frequently try to compensate. They tend to try to be more responsible or protective of those around them.

Whether or not a tragedy occurred is not as important as how the child interpreted the event. In other words, what decisions did the child make about life, self and others, i.e.., *"I decided it's not safe to get too close to the people I love because they might leave me."*

## QUESTIONS

Were there any tragedies in your family when you were a child? How did your parents respond? What did you decide about the tragedy?

## FAMILY VALUES

The values that both Mother and Father share are often developed by all the children in the family. (The exception to this rule is the "black sheep" who develops totally opposite values.) Example:

Sue's father was a partner in an oil company. Her mother was the owner of a clothing store.

Sue's family slogan would have been, *"You get ahead by working hard."* Sue now has difficulty balancing her work life with her social life.

## QUESTIONS

Ask yourself, If my family had a family slogan, what would it have been? How does it apply to you now?

## PARENTAL RESPONSE

Our values were also shaped by the way our parents responded to our behavior. If we skin our knee and Mom says, *"That must really hurt. What will you do about it?"* We are likely to develop a sense of self reliance. Whereas, if she makes a big fuss, takes care of the whole thing for us, and gets us an ice cream to make us feel better, then we may conclude that it pays to get hurt.

We are not suggesting that parents are to blame for how people think and feel. However, how we chose to interpret our parents' responses is important.

## QUESTIONS

Ask yourself: how did my parents respond to, or how did I expect my parents to respond to:

My being angry?
My school performance?
The way I expressed my opinions?
My not wanting to do what they wanted?
My sexual curiosity?
My friends?
My having fun?
My hobbies or lack of hobbies?
My spiritual life?
My eating habits?
The way I dressed?
My desire for possessions?

In many of the above examples, children may decide not to meet their parents' expectations because they feel "pushed" into doing it their parents' way. They may feel they can't meet their parents' expectations or they may fail at meeting their parents' expectations because of sibling competition, which was mentioned earlier.

## HOW DECISIONS MOLD OUR LIFE STYLE

Let's look at how our childhood decisions become the patterns we use for solving adult problems.

A child is born and has his first experience where life does not go his way. The child then makes a decision about that experience. A decision is defined by Webster as: a judgment or conclusion reached. For example:

Sharon was fourteen-months-old when she slipped while playing in a shallow pool of water. Her father saw she was in distress and pulled her out of the pool. Sharon was terrified. She decided life is dangerous, I can't handle things on my own. I need to have someone strong to help me out.

Notice how Sharon's decision is very accurate for the early situation. Sharon's decision then becomes an opinion. An opinion is defined by Webster as: *"a belief not based on absolute certainty or positive knowledge but on what seems true, valid or probable to one's own mind."* The problem with the decision becoming a belief or opinion is that it becomes set in your mind. Having opinions is useful and helpful. Having an outdated opinion is not useful.

Opinions then become expectations. Webster defines expectations as: to await; to look for as likely to occur or appear; anticipate. Sharon learns to expect that she can't handle things on her own, that she needs someone to help her out. She looks for and often creates situations that confirm her expectations.

## EXPECTATIONS

We often underestimate the power of expectation. In one of our classes we designed an exercise to make this point clearer:

The instructor sends one person, we'll call her Ann, out of the room. The rest of the group stands in a circle. Two people are chosen as "greeters". Their task is to greet Ann when she walks in the door and to bring her into the circle. The rest of the group is instructed to make Ann feel warm and welcome in a sincere way. The instructor invites Ann into the room and the "greeters" meet her and bring her into the group. The group usually does an excellent job of making Ann feel warm and welcome. The instructor sends Ann out of the room again and tells the group to do the exact same thing. The next time she enters the room, an amazing thing happens. When Ann walks in, the group starts being warm and welcoming but rapidly becomes distant and cold. Within ten seconds the group generally gets quiet and backs away from Ann.

What happened? Did Ann suddenly develop a case of bad breath? No. The group suggests that Ann was not as inviting the second time. She looked and acted more cautious. The first time her arms were loosely at her side. The second time she held her elbows tightly at her side. The first time her eyes glanced from person to person in a relaxed manner. The second time she looked suspiciously from one person to another. Why the change?

The instructor then asks Ann to share with the group what she was told before she entered the room on this second occasion. She reports, *"I was told the group might try to tickle me this time."*

The only difference between the first and second demonstrations was Ann's expectations. Ann had no idea that she had so much power to control the whole group's behavior.

We communicate our expectations very subtly by our body posture, our eye contact, by our tone of voice and by the words we choose to use. Usually, we provoke and get exactly what we expect.

## EARLY RECOLLECTIONS

Early recollections are tools for self understanding. Out of the millions of events which happen in our childhood, why do we choose to recall only a select few? Adler discovered that the early experiences we choose to keep in our awareness all have a consistent theme running through them. He concluded that we use this theme to maintain our life style convictions. Studying our early recollections can lead to self understanding.

To explain how to interpret memories we will look at four early recollections of an 18 year old female:

MEMORY #1
Age 2: *"Mother came in to patch me up and said, 'I told you you'd get hurt.' She had told me not to put my fingers in the fan but I was curious and didn't believe it would hurt because I couldn't see anything in there. I was surprised that it hurt."*

MEMORY #2
Age 5: *"I was being chased by a little boy and I lost my necklace."*

MEMORY #3
Age 6: *"Mother was making food. I thought it smelled like lamb chops and I said so. Mother said, 'No, it is steak.' So, I ate it. It tasted like lamb chops to me. I never ate steak any more after that."*

MEMORY #4
Age 6: *I was playing in a field at my favorite spot. I saw a bumble bee flying around. I didn't play there any more.*

## HOW TO INTERPRET RECOLLECTIONS

Out of the millions of experiences in this girl's childhood, why did she select these four incidents to cherish in her memory? On the surface they appear to be innocent.

84

However, if we consider the moral of the stories as if they are answers to the questions:
*"Life is...,"*
*"I am...,"*
*"Others are...,"*
*"So therefore...,"*
we can gain tremendous insight into what motivates her to make the decisions she makes.


## GUESSES

Let us look at each memory from this point of view. In this process we will examine the memories one at a time. We will make guesses to identify the life style theme, then modify the guesses as we collect more information.

MEMORY #1. Life is: dangerous, mysterious and surprising.
I am: unable to recognize danger.
Men are: ?
Women are: givers of advice.
So, therefore: I should trust the judgment of others over my own judgment.

At this point these are not conclusions but only our guesses. We must compare the answers to the other recollections and revise our guesses until there is a non-contradicting theme that runs throughout all of the memories. Any contradictions that we discover we will examine to help us find the consistent theme.

MEMORY #2. Life is: dangerous.
 I am: not in control.
 Men are: aggressive and dangerous.
 Women are: ?
So, therefore When I try to protect myself I lose.

MEMORY #3. Life is: surprising, unexpected and unpredictable.
I am: unable to trust my own judgment or anyone else's. ~

Men are: ?
Women are: unreliable advice givers.
So, therefore I can be safe by giving up and not participating at all.

At this point we can begin to see which guesses need to be revised and which ones are revealing a pattern. The word "unpredictable" fits well into the "life is" category of both memory #1, and #3, and is not contradicted by anything in #2. The "I am" answers all show a strong underestimation of her own judgment and her ability to control life. The only "men are" answers show men as dangerous and aggressive. However, women appear in two of the first three memories. Perhaps she sees them as more important.

The "women are" category of memory #3 shows that we must modify our "so, therefore" guess in memory #1. She cannot trust the judgment of others because she is unable to tell when their advice is helpful or harmful. The *"so, therefore, give up and don't participate"* theme is not repeated in #1 or in #2, but neither is it contradicted.

Let us look at memory #4 and see if these patterns are confirmed.

MEMORY #4. Life is: dangerous and unpredictable.
I am: unable to tell if things will be safe or dangerous.
Men are: ?
Women are: ?
So, therefore: I must give up forever what I want and protect myself by not participating.

If it were true that *"life was always dangerous and unpredictable, other people gave advice that was often unreliable and you couldn't trust your own judgment,"* who wouldn't withdraw and give up?

Notice in memory #4 that she does not even get stung by the bee. It is her expectation that causes her to give up and retreat.

## RECOLLECTIONS AND CURRENT PROBLEMS

Now, let's compare this girl's current life problems to see if her faulty opinion of life influences her decision making.

Problem 1: She could not find a boy friend. She was attractive and was often asked out by boys but she was so busy that she didn't have time to go on dates. On occasion, she would accept an invitation. However, something always would come up and she would have to cancel the date.

Problem 2: She wanted to become a commercial artist and had created many beautiful paintings; however, she would never show her paintings to anyone. She was unsure of whether they would like them.

Problem 3: She was a very talented musician and wanted to play with a group. However, she would only play alone in her room at home. She never let anyone hear her play. She wasn't sure if her playing was good enough.

We can see how this girl's life style prevented her from solving these problems. Her unrecognized doubts about her ability to distinguish a safe situation from an unsafe situation were causing her anxiety. She resolved this anxiety by using her favorite childhood solution - withdrawing and giving up. She was paralyzed by her faulty opinions about life.

As she became adept at recognizing her inappropriate way of relieving her anxiety, she started risking participation in spite of the fact that her feelings were telling her to withdraw. As she began to participate more, she was able to discover that she could do many things to deal with the unexpected challenges which she previously avoided. She discovered that she could take action to avoid being hurt without "losing her necklace." These successes gave her new courage which eventually made her anxiety disappear.

Being able to recognize your own prejudices and style, without condemning yourself, enables you to choose to either follow your style, or in situations where your style limits you, to courageously try new alternatives.

## YOUR MEMORIES

Try writing out your early memories or have a friend write out his. See if you can recognize the style. You may find that it is easier to recognize your friend's style than it is to recognize your own. This is because we are trying to see our own style looking through our own biases. Like the joke where the paranoid person claims, *"I am not paranoid! Everyone in the world really is after me!"*

As you will notice, each of the four recollections in the previous example tell about a specific incident. This is important! An early recollection cannot be considered significant if it is a generality. Example:

"A little boy always used to chase me."

This is a report, not an early recollection. It cannot be used in your interpretations.

"I was being chased by a little boy and I lost my necklace."

This is an early recollection. It describes a specific incident.

## TIPS ON INTERPRETING

Some tips to help you recognize the theme of early recollections are:

#1. Write out the answers to the "Life is...?" "Others are...?" "I am...?" "So therefore...? questions for each recollection and examine, discard or revise the contradictions.

#2. Write a "Newspaper headline" for each recollection. Example for recollection #3 above: **GIRL GIVES UP DUE TO INACCURATE ADVICE.**

#3. Consider the individual's *"position in the action"* in each recollection. Example for recollections above: #1 The victim when participating. #2 The retreater and the innocent victim. #3 The victim when participating. #4 The retreater.

#4. List the individual's current life problems and look for the consistent theme in the problems, then ask yourself what would have to be true about life to have that behavior make sense. Example: It would make sense to avoid dating, showing others your artwork or having them listen to your music if it were true that you could not count on your own judgment or the judgment of others.

## MEMORIES CHANGE

After therapy an individual's early memories change, revealing a new theme which is consistent with the changes the individual has made in therapy.

For example: A woman who came in for therapy because others were complaining that she was too vague, reported the following recollection:

*"I was in the farmyard. The pig chased me. I wasn't supposed to be there. I squeezed between the post and tank. I felt special because I outsmarted the pig."*

In our early sessions with this woman we could see why others felt that she was vague. When she would talk she would go on and on, using many pronouns.

*"Charley went with him and he took his time waiting for him until finally they couldn't wait any longer then he said that if Charley didn't hurry he would leave without him."*

When she would finally identify one of the pronouns we would suddenly realize that she was not talking about the person we had thought she was talking about. We were left with the same feeling that the pig had. That we couldn't pin her down. She was too vague.

After therapy her behavior changed and she was much more specific about things. When we asked her to tell us her recollection about the pig, she said:

*"I was in the barn lot. I looked up and I saw this old sow, which is a mother pig, I remember she was either taller or the same height as me. I didn't really feel afraid. I saw an opening between the tank and the fence. I ran through it, no, I squeezed through it. I felt good because I took care of myself."*

Notice how the moral of the story has changed. Instead of saying, *"I can be special by fooling others and not letting them pin me down."* it now says, *"I am resourceful and can take care of myself."*

## HOW MEMORIES MAINTAIN OUR STYLE

By keeping an awareness of certain selected experiences we actually are maintaining the flaws in our life style.

To outline the process of how we use early recollections to maintain our life style we can say:

### 1. FORMULATE LIFE STYLE
In childhood, after interpreting and assessing his predicament, the individual decides on a set of opinions to help him stay safe, belong and become significant. We refer to this set of opinions as his life style.

### 2. SELECT AND MODIFY MEMORIES
At some point in time after deciding on his style, the individual collects and modifies memories of experiences

90

which justify his opinions. These memories do not necessarily need to be consistent with reality. Often when comparing the recollections of two members of the same family we discover that they frequently have conflicting opinions of the same childhood event.

## 3. OFFSET THE LOGIC OF REALITY
The feelings created by these memories help to offset the challenges that the reality of everyday life places upon our opinions.

For example: Assume that Fred's childhood experiences have caused him to underestimate his ability to make sound judgments. The reality is that daily he will undoubtedly make many very good decisions. If he continued to concentrate on these successes, his self-concept (*"I have poor judgment"*) would be challenged. He would be forced, by his observation of reality to conclude, *"Maybe my judgment is better than I thought."* However, by maintaining memories which remind him of those childhood feelings of inadequacy, he can ignore the challenge of common sense and continue to justify his previous opinions. His private logic, as preserved by his early recollections, overrules common sense.

## 4. ACT ON FEELINGS
By maintaining our opinions in the form of feelings, we are allowed to avoid scrutinizing the logic of our convictions. Whenever the demands of the situation contradict our private logic we can ignore common sense and act on our feelings.

For example: The mistake in Andy's life style is: *"Love means not having to work. If others care about me, they will do it for me."* He is often unemployed. How does he justify his decision to avoid work? He may see an ad in the paper for a job as a construction worker, but due to his life style he may base his decision not to apply for the job on the fact that, *"I just don't feel like that type of job."*

Thus Andy is able to act on his feelings even though they don't make sense. He doesn't even have to justify his decision because it has been made without conscious awareness that he is making a choice.

## PRIORITIES

Early recollections and life style assessment help us to recognize the specific purpose of behavior. As a tool it gives us a general understanding of the purpose of behavior so we can consider a person's priorities.

To help us make a quick assessment, we can group an individual's actions into four major objectives. They are: feeling **significant**, being in **control**, being **comfortable**, or having others **pleased** with us. By observing the order of importance, or the priority, that an individual assigns to those objectives we can better understand the pattern of their behavior.

This priority theory in Adlerian psychology was first formulated in 1973 by Nira Kefir, an Israeli psychologist. In assigning a priority to these objectives we sometimes limit our flexibility. We do this by relying too heavily on only one objective. For instance, if we feel that we must always please, then we will run into trouble since no one can please others all the time. For example, we might have a boss who is critical and doesn't express much appreciation for what we have done. Let's take a look at some of the assets and some of the liabilities of each priority. Each person can use their priority in a useful or useless way.

## STRIVING FOR SIGNIFICANCE

If we exaggerate the importance of feeling significant or being better than others, we often try to impress others with how much we know and how capable we are at doing things. The price we often pay is that others feel inadequate around us. We often feel overburdened or overworked. We are often very willing to pay the price of being overworked in order to avoid feeling meaningless or worthless. People usually choose us when a difficult task needs to be done because we usually are responsible, knowledgeable, work hard and get things done. We use large words that display our authority on the subject.

## PLEASING

If we exaggerate the importance of pleasing others, we often judge our value by whether or not we are liked and by our ability to know and deliver what others want. We depend on compliments because we then know that someone is pleased with us. We often pay the price of not having many things our way and often feel resentful. We're willing to pay this price to avoid feeling rejected or criticized. Others are frequently pleased with us or feel irritated with us because we seldom directly ask for what we want. People enjoy being around us because we are very sensitive to others and say things that are pleasing to others. We sometimes avoid social situations because it is so much work to always guess what the others want.

## COMFORT

If we put to high a priority on being comfortable, we often exaggerate the demands that others put on us. We let them know this non-verbally by sighing. The price we pay for trying to be comfortable is that we often feel lazy and have a hard time getting started. Others are often irritated because we aren't doing our share. We are often willing to pay this price because we want to avoid stress and hassle. People enjoy being around us because we're usually easy-going and carefree.

## CONTROL

When we place too much importance on being in control, we often feel panicky when a situation arises where we aren't in control. We seldom allow others to become too close, so we pay the price of having social distance. We're willing to have that distance so no one can find where they might be able to embarrass or humiliate us. Occasionally, we adopt addicting habits such as alcohol or smoking for the purpose of proving that relinquishing control results in severe consequences. Some of our assets are that we are good leaders, are organized and like excitement.

Another priority we would like to suggest is the priority of moral significance. The feeling that we can be better than others if we are more morally proper than others. Often we are willing to pay the price of being someone's victim in order to achieve this goal. For example, the abused wife who says, *"Look how much he hurts me but I'm willing to stay together for the children's sake."* Or the alcoholic's spouse who stays in the marriage and is willing to endure all the discomfort in order to "help" his partner. One of their strengths is that they are willing to go out of their way to help others.

The other priority we'd like to add to this list is the priority of "having things" or "material possessions." The price we pay is the feeling of never being satisfied - always wanting more. However, we usually are very exciting and interesting to be with.

## PRIORITY CHART

On the following page is a priority chart to help you approximate what your priorities might be. The chart was designed by Bill Riedler. The information was taken from a lecture by Dr. William Pew and Miriam Pew M.S.W. A.C.S.W.

## Instructions:

Read the phrase at the top of each column. In the boxes under columns A, B, C and D, rate which phrase applies the closest to your situation. Mark a #1, #2, #3 or #4, one number in each box. #1 being the phrase that applies the most accurately to you, #4 being the phrase that applies to you the least accurately. Each square should contain a different number.

| | A | B | C | D | E |
|---|---|---|---|---|---|
| | How you see others: | How others may react to you: | What you try to avoid: | Your complaint about life: | YOUR PRIORITIES: |
| F | "I often feel others are testing me." | "Others often feel inadequate." | "I must avoid being meaningless or unimportant." | "I'm often overburdened." | SIGNIFICANCE |
| G | "Others are frequently inconsiderate." | "Others feel challenged by me when they state their opinions". | "I must avoid sudden humiliation." | "If I get too involved with others I can't do what I want." | CONTROL |
| H | "Others demand too much of me." | "Others feel irritated that I'm not doing my share." | "I must avoid stress." | "I have a hard time getting started or finishing things." | COMFORT |
| I | "Others are often in control." | "Others feel pleased but I feel resentful." | "I must avoid rejection and criticism." | "I seldom get a chance to see if my way works." | PLEASING |

After you have scored each square, add row F across, and put the total in the box under column E. Then add row G and put the total in the second box under row E. Repeat this same procedure for rows H and I.

If you have answered the questions honestly, the square under column E that has the lowest number represents the priority that you most often use. The square with the highest number in it is the priority that you use the least.

The purpose of this exercise is not to pigeon-hole you into one of these four categories, but is to help you recognize that you may be underestimating your ability to use other alternatives that are available to you.

The ideal priority, one that would ensure us of having the feeling of being worthwhile and assure us of the feeling of belonging would be the priority of having social interest. Social interest gives you the ability to look at what others want and what you want and come to some mutual agreement which meets the demands of the situation. This requires that we become adept at being cooperative, helpful, and able to enjoy participating. In the process of pursuing these goals there may be times when we can't be better than others, times when we must relinquish control, times when others will not be pleased with us and times when we must sacrifice our comfort. This requires flexibility. Once you become aware of someone's priority, there are many ways to enhance your ability to cooperate with them.

## I DON'T FEEL SIGNIFICANT

For example: Let's say your husband has the priority of significance. That means that he doesn't feel significant and believes that he needs to compensate. When he does this, by acting superior, your temptation is to cut him down to size because he makes you feel inadequate. However, if you do that it will only increase his need to prove to you that he is better than you.

He would be less inclined to make you feel inadequate if you use phrases like:

*"I'm having difficulty with . . . and I could sure use your help."*

*"You're right about that."*

*"That was a valuable suggestion."*

*"I learned a lot from your suggestion about.."*

These phrases should be sincere and honest. They are most effective if you are saying them from an equal position as opposed to a one-down position. The phrases work because he wants to prove to you that he is knowledgeable and valuable. If you let him know that you do feel that way about him, he has less need to prove it.

This person often does more than his share of the work. It is tempting to think, *"Oh, I'll give that job to John. He'll get the job done."* It is essential not to exploit his feeling that *"I'm important when I do more than my share."* As a result of this feeling, he frequently doesn't know his own limits. He takes on tasks beyond what the average person would, thinking he can handle it. He often minimizes the consequences he suffers (i.e., family complaints that he's never around, or feeling so "burned out" that when he does have time off he vegetates in front of the TV.).

## COMFORT MEANS LOVE

This individual equates comfort with love. Whenever you interfere with his comfort he assumes that you don't love him. Limit the demands you place on this person. When you do make a demand make it thorough, complete, and within the individual's ability. It should be thorough and complete so that you don't have to approach him with another demand in order to complete the first task. Set up as many situations as possible where, if he doesn't do his share, he will suffer from his own consequences as opposed to you having to hassle him. Other people tend to take up the slack for this person and in this way he never has to suffer any consequences. This only confirms his feeling that if he doesn't get it done someone else will. If he is on staff other members should be instructed not to do his work. Even if they could do a better job or do it faster. Make use of this person's ability to find short cuts on projects.

If you have a project to be done, give him as much time as possible. You may want to have check points in the process where you review what he has completed. This makes it more difficult for him to put the project off until the last minute and helps him avoid the pressures of meeting deadlines.

He is an expert at creating excuses for not getting things done. The more you accept his excuses, the more excuses he will create. This person feels important by avoiding demands. He feels, *"Love means that others don't put demands on me."* When you complain that he is not doing his share, it makes him feel lazy. This only confirms his fears and thus perpetuates the problem.

## I MUST BE PLEASING

This person feels that he will not be important if anyone is displeased with him, and therefore is usually willing to help anyone at any time in any way possible. He can only escape these extreme social demands by limiting social contact. As was mentioned earlier, blame or criticism are devastating to this person. So if the person is working for you, and has made a mistake, it is effective to approach the problem from, *"I need your help in improving this situation."* as opposed to *"You did this wrong..."*

This individual has a hard time saying *"no"*. He often says *"yes"* and resents it. This resentment often shows up as mistakes. If you are the employer, it is helpful to make it clear in many ways that it is OK for him to say *"no"* - that you won't get angry or be disappointed.

Make use of this person's sensitivity to others and their ability to make strangers feel welcome and comfortable. This individual hints at what he wants as opposed to directly saying what he wants. As a result, he frequently doesn't get what he wants nor does he find out how good his ideas are. He therefore has a low opinion of himself. You can be helpful to him by listening for and acknowledging his hints, no matter how feeble or unassertive they are. Carry out some of his suggestions and show him how helpful or valuable they where If you do this, you will increase his productivity, decrease his mistakes and help him become more assertive.

## I DON'T HAVE ENOUGH CONTROL

This person feels that only those in control are respected. He also believes that he doesn't have control often enough to win your respect. The most effective way to deal with a person who has a control priority is to give him several options that you are also willing to go along with. For example, if this person is working for you, you would want to give him the bottom line of what you want to accomplish and let him figure out and control how to get there. If you don't use this process you will often run into a battle. Frequently this person will agree with you regarding a task, then turn around and do it his way.

Give this person tasks that require leadership and organization.

Don't try to corner or pin this person down.

If this person is your employer, avoid unpleasant surprises, since he likes to feel in control or *"on top of things."* When he feels powerless he may try to regain his power by being angry. It is best not to be intimidated by his anger nor to do anything to make him feel more powerless.

## THE PROCESS OF CHANGE

After becoming more aware of your life style and your priorities, you may have decided that you would like to make some changes. The following is a six step process of how change occurs:

### 1. Recognize or admit that you have a problem.

Often we don't admit that we have a problem. We ignore or numb ourselves to the pain we feel. We do this because we are afraid to change. Even though our patterns may get us into trouble, they are at least familiar. We have no idea what it would be like to change those well-protected patterns so we resist. Especially since the old patterns seem so essential to us.

### 2. Identify the price you pay for your behavior.

One of the ways to help you decide whether or not you want to change a behavior pattern is to look at the price you pay for continuing the behavior. Here is an example:

Bob recognized that he had a pattern of proving that he knew more than others. This made the people around him feel inadequate. He realized that the price he was paying was that he seldom let people that they might find out that he didn't know all the answers. He also realized that by having all the answers, he was missing out on the contributions of his staff. He also got in touch with the discomfort of the pressure he felt to *"know it all."*

### 3. Decide that you want to change.

This step sounds so easy but is the most difficult of all. We think we want to change the behavior and have all the understanding but we still resist.

### 4. Understand the purpose of your pattern of behavior.

Have you ever thought, *"I must be crazy for acting this way?"* This step makes the behavior understandable so that you don't feel crazy. Once you understand the purpose of the behavior it is less threatening.

### 5. Recall situations in the past where you used the pattern.

Recall recent situations where you have used the pattern. It is helpful when changing a pattern to become as familiar with it as possible. This will help to expedite the change.

### 6. Recognize that you now have a choice as to whether or not you want to continue the behavior.

You will find that either the behavior pattern will disappear or you will catch yourself in the midst of your pattern. You will then have a choice.

You may decide that you want to use your old pattern. That's OK. The important issue is that you will no longer feel like the victim of circumstances.

The following is an example of the process of change:

Susan recognized that she had a pattern of feeling left out in groups of three or more people.

When she examined the situation closer she recognized that as a child, things would go well until a third person would come along. Then, since younger children are frequently considered *"tag along"*, the person that she was with gave more attention to the third person. This often meant that Susan was left behind. Susan interpreted the situation as: *"I'm not important to be with. Even if people choose to be with me it will only be until someone really important comes by and then I'll be left behind."*

Susan identified that the price she paid for choosing this pattern was that she didn't really allow anyone to get too close to her. She thought it would be much less painful to not get close than to experience the pain of having that person leave her for someone else. She missed out on the richness close friendships would have added to her life. Susan felt very alone. She numbed herself to the loneliness she felt by working many long hours. She also paid the price of feeling too dependent on the few people she would allow to be close to her. She felt uncomfortable with her degree of possessiveness of those people.

After Susan became aware of the problem and realized where it originated, she could reflect on many situations where she had allowed that to happen in the past. She got to the point where she caught herself just as she was about to create the situation and made a choice not to continue. She was aware that her opinion of herself was inaccurate and a limitation to the enjoyment of her life.

Caution: Frequently when a person has not decided to change, they create what we call *"reconfirming behavior."* Reconfirming behavior is when you are in the middle of your pattern and you decide to do something different. However, you set up the situation to back-fire so that you can say *"See what happens when I try to do something different. That proves that I don't dare to change!"* For example:

Ellen realized that she did everything possible to please people so that they would like her. However she didn't like all the resentment she felt. Nor did she like the fact that so many people took advantage of her. So the next time her boss told her to get him coffee, she said, *"Get your own @!#&@! coffee."* At which point her boss blew up. Ellen said to herself, *"See what happens when I try to assert myself! It just isn't worth it!"*

Ellen's clumsy method of asserting herself reconfirmed her mistaken idea that she must always please others. others.

# *Chapter Four*

# OUR SOCIAL SITUATION

### Factors Of Unpreparedness

We can get a better understanding of ourselves and others if we consider human problems as being caused by our lack of preparation to meet upcoming challenges. There will always be challenges in life. From time to time things will go in your favor, then go against you, creating challenges. However, these challenges do not become problems until we feel unprepared. We can group the factors that contribute to our unpreparedness into four categories:

**1. Faulty life style convictions.**

**2. Insufficient social interest.**

**3. Lack of information or skill.**

**4. Pressures from our social situation.**

In a previous chapter we discussed the life style factor. The last chapter of this book will deal with the implications of social interest.

Factor number 3, lack of information or skill, is perhaps the first and only factor considered when most people experience difficulties in their life. Ironically, this factor is the least likely source of the problem!

"What's wrong with you? Don't you know that you shouldn't do things like that!" This exclamation infers that the only reason you did the wrong thing is that you lacked information. This is seldom the case.

Occasionally we are lacking information; however, when such is the case we do not feel emotionally devastated by the problem. If you are feeling desperate, confused, or if you feel resigned to put up with the problem, it is a clue that it is one of the other factors that is limiting you. If it were only a lack of information you would recognize your deficiency and begin reading, studying and discussing the situation - moving closer to a solution. You would enjoy the learning process as opposed to feeling desperate.

Of course, as you change the faulty notions in your life style there will be a need for new information. You can gain these new skills by reading chapter five on assertiveness and conflict solving skills.

This chapter will be devoted to clarifying factor number four, revising our social situation. We will discuss how our rapidly changing social situation has affected our ability to live together, work together and love together.

## THE MODEL CITIZEN

How would you prepare a child so that when grown, he would become a model citizen in a country that was ruled by a dictator? What characteristics would you want that child to develop? Would you want those same characteristics in a child that was living in a democracy?

Consider the two lists on the following page. The characteristics listed in the left column are ones we see useful for living under a dictator in an autocratic setting. The characteristics listed in the right column are what we see as essential to make democracy effective.

Notice that the two columns are almost opposite in nature. Our current predicament is that, legally, we live in a democracy. However, few of us have been raised to have the characteristics necessary to be responsible citizens in such a setting.

We have written an entire book, Redirecting Children ' s Behavior, outlining in detail how to revise parenting techniques in order to foster democratic characteristics in our children. We won't go into those details here. We do wish to explore how our autocratic traditions not only prevent the development of democracy, but also actually interfere with mental health. As you read the lists on the next page ask yourself which characteristics did your parents seem to be trying to develop in you.

# COMPARISON CHART

| AUTOCRATIC CITIZEN | DEMOCRATIC CITIZEN |
|---|---|
| Obedient. | Responsible. |
| Doesn't wonder why. | Asks why. Feels a sense of responsibility to the demands of the situation. |
| Fearful - responds to fear. | Encouraged and encouraging. |
| Follower. | Makes decisions WITH others. |
| Passive. | Assertive. |
| Domineering to those under him, obedient to those over him. | Can be either a leader or a follower based upon the demands of the situation, without fear of losing status. |
| Feels like a sinner. | Has a sense of equality and self-worth. |
| Lacks self respect - obeys others. | Has ability to influence others. |
| Fear of losing status by making mistakes limits his creativeness. | Has the courage to be imperfect which fosters creativity. |
| Knows what is right and wrong according to the dictator. | Takes the time to understand the situation before passing judgment. |
| Dependent - independent | Interdependent |
| Only says "no" when prepared to fight. | Says "no" openly as a tool to promote agreement. |
| Takes orders. | Takes responsibility. |
| Agrees regardless of desires, then complains. | Votes, then holds representatives responsible. |

## SPARE THE ROD

It appears that in the past our culture was subtly refined, over hundreds of years, to foster a consciousness of submission. A slave mentality. Many concepts which were originally devised to promote cooperation were gradually misinterpreted and misrepresented to serve the needs of a system advocating that cooperation could only be achieved through control. Even religious teachings were gradually misinterpreted to justify the concept that some individuals had the divine right to dominate and control others.

Parenting principles such as *"spare the rod, spoil the child"* were eventually distorted resulting in the development of children that had a willingness to allow other people to rule their lives.

What was originally meant by the saying, *"spare the rod, spoil the child"?* A colleague of ours, Dr. Oscar Christensen, had a group of religious educators explore the origin of the saying. Their findings were that the saying was making a reference to the tools used by the shepherds. In Biblical times, the shepherds used primarily two tools, the rod and the staff. The staff was the tool with the hook on the end, used to restrain the sheep by hooking him around the neck. The rod, was a straight stick used to guide the flock. If a sheep strayed to the left, the shepherd would use the rod and gently apply pressure to the side of the sheep, guiding him back into line.

Thus, we can say that *"spare the rod, spoil the child"* really means, *"You must provide GUIDANCE or you will spoil your child."* Somehow most of us were led to believe that this phrase meant, *"Hit your child with the rod or you will spoil him."* How absurd! Can you imagine what would happen if the shepherd would use the rod to hit the straying sheep? Not only would the straying sheep run away, but also the entire flock would scatter!

How did this phrase get misinterpreted? Perhaps those that wished to dominate and control others used the misinterpretation to justify their own use of punishment and fear. Torture and intimidation were common tools of ruling tyrants. If they could justify to the masses that *"The Almighty"* condoned their methods they increased their chances of gaining the citizen's willingness to submit. Also, if the rulers could be successful in convincing the masses to spank their children, then the young would develop both a fear of punishment and an attitude that would make war seem logical. The child would be raised to believe that hurting others is a way to get them to do what you want them to do. When older, those children would not challenge the dictator's command to go to war for the purpose of taking the possessions of weaker communities.

We are not claiming that the rulers consciously manipulated the masses and schemed and plotted with the idea of misleading the young. The rulers, too, were victims of the flaws in the social system. The misleading ideas just evolved. The misinterpretations were not conscious plans. When we read the Bible or any other material our natural tendency is to look harder for the ideas that will justify what we are already doing than to look for ideas to help us change and improve. We are more inclined to try to maintain a clear conscience than to challenge our own thinking.

## THE TRADITIONAL FAMILY

Today many relationships are being disturbed because we have changed from an autocratic to a democratic form of living together, without simultaneously changing our autocratic attitudes. As we continue to revise our parenting methods we will move toward a much more effective democracy, but meanwhile we must find solutions to the problems of how to make democracy work with a generation of people who were raised to underestimate their own power and overestimate their need for a generous benefactor.

The following three scenarios may clarify the effects of the social changes we are experiencing.

## ONE OR MORE GENERATIONS AGO:

The MAN of the house is returning home after work and the LITTLE LADY greets him at the door.

Tom:      *I'm home.*

Judy:     *Hi honey, how was your day?*

Tom walks past her and plops down in HIS chair and says:
          *Where's my paper?*

Judy:     *Here it is honey.*

Tom, snapping his fingers:
          *Get me some coffee.*

Tom, as Judy brings the coffee:
          *Well?*

Judy:     *Well what?*

Tom:      *Well, what's for dinner?*

Judy:     *I was thinking of having roast beef and corn.*

Tom, in an angry voice:
          *Now listen here woman, you know I don't like corn!*

Judy:     *Oh I'm sorry honey, what would you like?*

Tom:      *Make roast beef and string beans. How soon will it be ready?*

Judy:       *In about 20 minutes.*

Tom:        *You could have had it ready when I got home. I've been working hard all day trying to provide for this family. That's the least you could do. How were the kids today?*

Judy:       *Johnny's been picking on his sister again and I told him you'd take care of it when you got home.*

Tom:        *I don't know what I'm going to do with those kids. JOHNNY GET IN HERE!! What's this I hear that you've been picking on your sister again? Answer me young man!*

Johnny:     *But dad she.....*

Tom:        *Don't talk back to me!*

Tom, while spanking Johnny:
            *How many times have I told you that it's not nice to hit people?*

Judy:       *Honey, don't be so hard on him.*

Let's consider what convictions Johnny might develop after living in the above environment for 21 years. Remember, Johnny feels small and wants to get to be mature. The big people seem to get all the privileges. As he grows Johnny is desperately trying to become a REAL MAN. What would be his answers to the following questions?

*Q.       What is a REAL man like?*

*A.        A real man is the boss. He is tough and is the provider. Everyone else needs him so much that they give him whatever he wants. No one is as important as the man of the house.*

*Q.*     *How does a woman treat a REAL man?*

*A.*     *When the man says "jump" the woman says "How high?" on the way up .*

*Q.*     *Can I really become a REAL man?*

*A.*     *I'm not sure. I sure feel pretty helpless compared to my daddy.*

We can also imagine that Johnny's sister may be forming some opinions about herself and the role of a woman.

*Q.*     *What is required of a Real woman?*

*A.*     *She must be willing and able to submit.*

*Q.*     *How good is a woman's judgment?*

*A.*     *Not very good at all. Even the job of caring for the children, which she has been trained for ever since she played with dolls, has to be "handled" by the man. (I told him you'd take care of it when you got home.)*

*Q.*     *Is the woman's role something to look forward to?*

*A.*     *Absolutely not! It won't take much convincing from the woman's movement to get me to fight for more rights for women.*

## A GENERATION LATER

Johnny is growing up and is setting about the task of proving that he is a REAL MAN. He has picked himself a *"little woman"* and is just coming home from work. However, there is one important change. It is a generation later and that *"little woman"* has been reading *"Ms. Magazine"!* Watch what happens.

John, as he walks in the door after work:
*Hi, I'm home.*

Sue: *What's for dinner?*

John: *What do you mean, what's for dinner? That's women's work. What have you been doing all day; watching TV and eating bon boons?*

Sue: *Listen buster, don't give me that smart talk!*

John: *Well I've been working all day. I'm the one who brings home the bacon around here. The least you could do is to have dinner ready for me.*

Sue: *Well I'm writing this article on child abuse and I'm bringing home more money than you this month. So what's for dinner?*

John, in a voice weak with resignation:
*Well, all right I guess. What do you want me to make?*

Sue, with indignation:
*Do you always have to be such a wimp! Can't you just make a decision? Why do you always have to ask me?*

## WHAT DISTURBED THE RELATIONSHIP?

This relationship is obviously disturbed. However, the cause of the disruption is not that John and Sue don't love each other. It is the product of the changing social situation. It is the result of taking two people with autocratic training and expecting them to function in a democratic setting.

Notice that John disturbs the relationship simply by trying to do what he feels will win Sue's love and admiration; he tries to be a REAL MAN. Sue, responding to the current atmosphere of equality, is trying to avoid being bossed. However, she has never seen a model of how two people can live together with mutual respect. She has only the model of a hierarchy to draw upon. She does not want to be dominated, but instead of co-operating, she dominates. She says, *"I must not be on the bottom, so I'll be on top!"* However, remember that she, because of the model she observed while growing up, underestimates herself and doubts her ability to make sound judgments. Therefore, when she succeeds in cutting John down, to keep him from dominating, she complains that he is a *"wimp."* Her self-doubt misleads her to believe that she needs a *"STRONG MAN."*

We call these mixed feelings a *"double bind."* He is also caught in a double bind. On one hand he wants her to be assertive and on the other he feels the need to be the dominant one.

## LOVE WITH MUTUAL RESPECT

There are few places we can look to see a model of how to live together with mutual respect. All of our tradition is based upon the notion of determining *"who will be the boss of whom?"* In the past, the order of command was well defined. First there was God. (Occasionally many authority figures of lower status claimed that His power was for the purpose of enforcing their dictates. *"Do as I say because even if I don't catch you, God is always watching.)* After God came man, then the woman, then the first born son, then the other children, then the dog, followed by the cat, the mouse and so on. Everyone knew his role and there was a certain comfort in that. Today most of us are uncertain of our role.

We are all social pioneers assigned with the task of creating a new model of love with mutual respect. It is our challenge to break free of our tradition and define and demonstrate new principles of living together.

Through doing our counseling work together as a team and by collecting ideas from others during our lecture tours, we have been attempting to more clearly formulate that model. We offer the following scenario, not as the optimum model, but as a collection of suggestions. We hope they will stimulate your thinking so that together we can provide future generations with a better model.

## A NEW MODEL

John is just returning from work. (It may be, however, that John has elected to care for the children and Sue is the one returning from work.)

John:     *Hi, honey, I'm home.*

Sue:      *Hi, dear. How was your day?*

John:     *I'm really beat. What's for dinner?*

Sue smiles and places her hand on John's arm and looks at him without saying anything.

John:     *I put you down again, didn't I?*

Sue:      *Yes. Looks like neither of us feel like cooking tonight.*

John:     *What I would like to do is to go out to dinner at a real fancy restaurant tonight.*

Sue:      *That would be fun, but I'm writing this article on child abuse. I want to get it done tonight. How about we just go to a quick food place?*

John:     *I'm unwilling to go to a quick food place because I really worked hard today and I feel real entitled. What do you need to do on the article?*

114

Sue:      *I want to edit and type the final draft.*

John:      *I could borrow the neighbor's typewriter and we could both type. I'll bet we could finish it in half the time.*

Sue:      *Great! Then afterwards we could go out.*

John:      *I'd prefer to go out first, have a nice relaxing dinner and then come home and work on the article.*

Sue:      *I'd be willing to do that as long as you agree that we return home by seven o'clock.*

John:      *Sure, that would be no problem.*

Sue and John, together
      *OK, Lets do it!*

## HOW THEY AVOIDED CONFLICT

Let's examine the principles that John and Sue used to solve their conflicts.

John:      *Hi, honey, I'm home.*

Sue:      *Hi, dear. How was your day?*

Both John and Sue are expressing care and affection for each other as opposed to *"coming out fighting"* as they did in the second example.

John:      *I'm really beat. What's for dinner?*

Sue smiles and places her hand on John's arm and looks at him without saying anything.

When John starts putting Sue into her traditional role Sue recognizes that he is only acting that way because of his training. She doesn't see it as if John was saying, *"You're not important to me."* Instead of a hostile reaction she, nonverbally, communicates to him that she loves him even though he has just put her down.

This firm, but kind pressure helps John recognize his own mistake. She did not make him feel defensive.

John:      *I put you down again, didn't I?*

John avoids the temptation to get defensive. Whenever you catch yourself getting defensive and trying to justify why you have behaved in a certain way, then you know that you are preventing the possibility of sensible discussion of your differences. You are disturbing the equality of the relationship by putting yourself down.

Sue:       *Yes. Looks like neither of us feel like cooking to-night.*

Here Sue defines the demands of the situation. This directs their attention away from their individual inadequacies and focuses them on what they each must do to find a solution. Their personal worth is not challenged.

John:      *What I would like to do is to go out to dinner at a real fancy restaurant tonight.*

John tells Sue his preference. Without this information, Sue can not find alternative solutions. We have been trained NOT to talk about what WE want. Traditionally when we wanted something we had to disguise our desires as if we wanted only to do something for the other person. When talking to the King you would not just tell him you wanted more land, you would say, *"If you would give me more land, your Majesty, then I could grow more wheat for you."*

Sue:       *That would be fun, but I'm writing this article on child abuse. I want to get it done tonight. How about we just go to a quick food place?*

Sue communicates that John's idea is acceptable to her and explains the reason for her reluctance to agree. Then she suggests an alternative plan.

John:      *I'm unwilling to go to a quick food place .....*

John calmly states what he is unwilling to do. Again, this provides essential information for finding alternatives *"I'm unwilling"* is another phrase that we seldom use because of our traditional training. Can you imagine what would happen if the loyal subject said to his king, *"Your Majesty I'm unwilling to do that."* Or, *"Sergeant, I'm unwilling..."* The only way you could be unwilling is if you had a bigger army and were prepared to fight. Saying, *"I'm unwilling"* was an invitation to war.

John: .    *because I really worked hard today and I feel real entitled. What do you need to do on the article?*

Here John is not ashamed to admit his imperfections. He is not ashamed to be himself, which creates an atmosphere of openness which is conducive to problem solving. He also asks questions so that he better understands Sue's desires.

Sue:      *I WANT to edit and type the final draft.*

Notice that Sue says, *"I WANT"* instead of saying, *"I NEED."* She is modeling self respect. She is communicating that she feels comfortable about her desires. Had she said *"NEED"*, it would have been as if she had said, *"It is my duty to give up whatever I want and do whatever you want, except I NEED to edit the article just as I NEED to breathe. Without it I would die."* Need is often used as a sneaky way to say *"no"* without making it look like you are being defiant. It also communicates that you are afraid to say *"no"* to the other person.

117

John:      *I could borrow the neighbor's typewriter and we could both type. I'll bet we could finish it in half the time.*

John is now talking about what COULD be done. Often we concentrate more on what can't be done. By avoiding the use of *"I can't"* he is creating excitement about their teamwork.

Sue:       *Great! Then afterwards we could go out.*

Notice Sue's enthusiasm about coming to an agreement. By being enthusiastic she is encouraging both John and herself to find a solution to the problem. Had she been negative, *"I'm not going anywhere until I'm done!"* or indifferent, *"Oh, I don't care. Do what you want."* then she would have disrupted the problem solving process.

John:      *I'd prefer to go out first, have a nice relaxing dinner and then come home and work on the article.*

John again expresses his preferences. They are both careful not to allow the other person to hurt them. If they were to give in to something that they were unsatisfied with, the result would be feelings of resentment. They would not be participating with full enthusiasm. By expressing preferences they are moving toward agreement.

Sue:       *I'd be willing to do that as long as you agree that we return home by seven o'clock.*

John:      *Sure, that would be no problem.*

Sue describes the conditions under which she would be WILLING to agree. She does not try to guess what John wants or doesn't want. That is his job Nor does she expect that John should know what she wants she tells him.

Sue and John, together:
       *OK, Let's do it!*

118

Now they have come to AGREEMENT! They have not compromised. The end result of a compromise is two losers. In a compromise, both parties give in. Afterwards each concentrates more on the half they had to give up than on the half they gained. Sue and John, by the use of these principles, have strengthened their relationship. As a review here is a list of the principles they used:

## 18 STEPS TO AGREEMENT

1. Express care and affection.

2. Use silent, kind firmness.

3. Avoid making the other person feel defensive.

4. Avoid being defensive.

5. Define the demands of the situation.

6. Tell your preferences.

7. Tell the other person which ideas are acceptable.

8. Explain the reasons for any reluctance to agree.

9. Suggest alternative plans.

10. Calmly state what you are unwilling to do.

11. Admit your imperfections.

12. Ask questions to better understand the other person's desires.

13. Tell the other person what you want, not what you need.

14.  Discuss what COULD be done, not what can't be done.

15.  Don't give in, allowing the other person to hurt you.

16.  Describe the conditions under which you are willing to agree.

17.  Don't try to guess what the other person wants, ask.

18.  Don't compromise, promote agreement.

## DEMOCRACY STIMULATES MENTAL HEALTH

When we look back at our more autocratic predecessors we get the impression that most of them were willing to submit to the dictates of others. Seemingly, they had the ability to subordinate their desires to the wishes of authority figures.

However, if we look more closely at the situation we discover that this was not the case. People did not submit. They just rebelled by claiming illness and limitation. We see that autocratic living or working conditions foster mental illness.

In an autocratic setting it is not socially acceptable to be assertive or to say *"no"* openly. The method that individuals developed to solve this problem was to become inadequate. In that way they could do what they wanted, still claim good intentions and keep a clear conscience.

They did not just pretend to be inadequate, which would only fool the others. They actually arranged to feel inadequate, even deceiving themselves - leaving their conscience unchallenged. The severity of their claims of inadequacy ranged from making careless mistakes to becoming psychotic. Physical inadequacies ranged from a simple headache to death.

Instead of saying, *"No, I don't feel like it tonight,"* the woman would say, *"I have a headache."* When an individual was unwilling to meet the demands of the situation by getting a job, choosing a mate or being co-operative, he would not openly admit his reluctance. To do that would reveal his defiance and lead to a loss of status. Instead he would develop neurotic symptoms to explain and justify his unwillingness. *"I won't"* was totally unacceptable, but *"I can't"* was the road to freedom. *"If only I didn't have this chronic allergy, then I could risk finding a job."*

## I CAN'T DRIVE

Occasionally we find that a phobia is used as a way to disguise defiance.

One young woman came for counseling to overcome her phobia of driving. She had been raised in a very autocratic family and her father had been very domineering.

She had married a very gentle man, but he had been raised to feel loved when women waited on him and did whatever he requested.

She was very dedicated to serving him. He would hint and she would make special trips to the store just to get whatever he requested for dinner. Although she was accommodating, she resented his subtle domination.

He wanted to have children. She told him that she, too, would like to have a child but her fear of driving would make it impossible for her to care for an infant. He asked her to get counseling to overcome her phobia.

In our early sessions we did not discuss her fear. Instead we helped her to become more assertive with her husband. We helped her recognize how she felt obligated. She developed the skills of how to say *"no"* in a friendly way

121

and to negotiate solutions that were agreeable to both her and her husband.

After her ability to openly get what she wanted had improved, she reported that she was no longer feeling so dominated by her husband. We then brought up the subject of her phobia about driving. We showed her how her fear was her way to be secretly defiant. We suggested that she give driving another try and told her to see if she still had the same feelings.

Two months later we met with her again. She reported that she was no longer afraid to drive. She also informed us that she had told her husband that she was not yet ready to have children. They discussed their differences and came to an agreement to wait one year and then discuss the topic again.

The phobic symptoms had disappeared because in the new, more democratic family atmosphere, symptoms were no longer needed. Democracy stimulated her mental health.

If you are suffering from a phobia we would suggest that you ask yourself the question, *"What would be different if I was not afraid?"* The answer to that question may lead you to recognize the PURPOSE of your phobia.

## MATCHING ATTITUDES WITH FREEDOM

Even though the freedom offered to us through democracy tends to stimulate mental health we are still not in the position to take advantage of all of these benefits. This is because most of us were not raised to have the mental attitudes necessary to make democracy effective. We have not matched our attitudes with the legal freedom available to all of us. We are social pioneers, struggling between democracy and autocracy.

We will not be able to realize the joy and satisfaction of our democratic freedom until we develop democratic attitudes. We legally have *"government by the people."* However, we the citizens, don't do our part. The majority does not become familiar with the issues. The majority doesn't even vote! The majority does not meaningfully discuss the issues with their neighbors, reach consensus, communicate its choices to the representatives and then hold the representatives responsible. We complain about not having responsible government, however the real problem is that we are not responsible citizens.

If we were to become responsible, we might establish a formal system to record a candidate's election promises and remove from office those who, without permission, strayed from their promises.

This lack of responsibility on our part is because we were not raised to participate in the decision making. Many of us were told, *"Yours is not to wonder why. Yours is but to do or die."* It is our challenge to develop, in ourselves, those badly needed characteristics.

We have changed to the point where we are unwilling to abide by, or accept, the dictates of anyone. Children today no longer see a model of mother being willing to submit unconditionally to father. However, we have not developed our confidence in our own abilities nor our ability to co-operate to the point where we can truly become interdependent. We tend to vacillate between dependence, *"I need you"* and independence, *"I don't need anyone."*

The promise of dictators is, *"Give me all the control and responsibility and I'll take care of all your problems for you."* Unfortunately, this promise is almost identical to what most children experience as they are growing up. Mom and dad have all the control and take care of all the problems. *"I don't want you playing with Johnny. He'll get you into trouble."*

So we see two attitudes in effect:

*"I don't want anyone telling me what to do."*

and:

*"I need someone to take care of my problems for me."*

These attitudes put a tremendous strain on those who are trying to run our government. On one hand, we are all complaining about government regulations and criticizing their inefficiency. While on the other hand we are desperately striving to get the government to solve our problems for us. We complain about taxes while we're trying to figure out what we can do to get a government grant.

## SOMETHING FOR NOTHING

Whenever you expect the government to give you a grant or some type of aid you are asking them to force your neighbors to pay for something that they may not want. You're telling party number one (the government) to take (not earn), money from party number two (your neighbor) and spend it on behalf of party number three (you).

This indirect process automatically guarantees that:

The money, since it does not belong to the party who is spending it and is not being spent to benefit the party who is spending it, will be spent with a diminished concern for value and quality .

The transaction will require more non productive administrative labor. (Needs assessments and program evaluations.)

The person who unwillingly has to relinquish the funds will feel resentful. (The taxpayer.)

You will be unsatisfied with what the government gives you and resentful of their demands to control how you use it.

The end result is that the government must take more and more money from you and your neighbor to be able to continue to give you (for free?) the things you want. This spiraling inefficiency leads to economic problems.

This striving to get something for nothing not only creates problems in our economy, it also robs you of the satisfaction of feeling worthwhile. Striving to get something for nothing is an indication that you are underestimating both your true value and your ability to achieve, on your own, what you want.

## I'LL DO IT FOR YOU

Shortly after working with Kath Kvols to self-published the book, Redirecting Children's Behavior, we received a letter from one of the editors of "Psychology Today" Magazine. His letter said that he had read our book. He wanted to know if we were interested in having it published nationally. We called him and set up an appointment to visit him. He was extremely encouraging. He told us that, after reading our book, he felt that it could very easily be a best seller. He knew a major book publishing company and would be happy to take our book to them to see if they wanted to publish it nationally.

When we left his office we were ecstatic. We went out and celebrated. In fact it was probably one of the happiest moments in our lives!

BUT... It didn't last.

Prior to this happy moment we had been really working to get more people to read our book. Each day we would come up with new ideas of how to reach more people. We were constantly involved in one project after another. Calling on book stores, getting on TV and radio shows, giving lectures, sending out letters, making phone calls. Some projects were successful, others failed. However, the challenges had been adding flavor to our lives. Three months later we were still waiting for the editor to *"make our book into a best seller."* We weren't overly anxious because we knew that these things take time. However, we suddenly realized that the last three months had given us a very empty feeling. We had become grouchy and irritable and we weren't having much fun.

We were waiting for someone to *"DO IT FOR US."* We realized that we had stopped working! We were waiting for the new publisher to come along and take care of all our problems. The excitement was missing from our lives. We missed all the projects and challenges.

We looked at the records and realized that our book sales had dropped from 120 copies per month down to 60 copies a month! Prior to that time they were growing steadily every month.

We decided to stop looking for something for nothing. We did not yet know if the big publisher was going to take over our book or not, but we figured, *"Why should anyone else invest in our book if we are unwilling to."*

We went back to work as if we had never heard anything about anyone doing something for us. We took the attitude that we, on our own, were going to make our book so popular that we would help the big publisher - not depend upon him helping us. WE wanted to get the joy of being the useful party.

After another three months the *"Psychology Today"* editor called us and told us that the big publisher really liked our book. However, they had just published another book on the topic of parenting. We weren't even disappointed. By that time our own sales efforts were really paying off.

We are to the point now where every day we get book orders from all over North America. Last month we sold 1,047 copies. It's not the best seller yet, but we're working on it. However, we have realized that there is something far more important - our progress toward that goal is a measurement of what WE are doing. It makes US feel worthwhile.

From time to time I forget the lesson I learned from the *"Psychology Today"* editor and I start looking for someone to take care of me. Or I start blaming others for my mistakes. However, accepting the responsibility for our own happiness feels so much more rewarding. It is my hope that you will join me in this challenge to take on more responsibility in order to make democracy more effective.

# *Chapter Five*

# ASSERTIVE CONFLICT SOLVING

### Assertiveness

A s we explained in the first chapter, many factors of our childhood combine to influence the way in which we interact wih others when we become adults.

One of the factors to consider is that most of us were raised by parenting methods that our parents learned from their parents, and their parents used techniques they had learned from our grandparents.

This presents a problem because in most cases grandparents were not raising children to prepare them for living in a democracy. They, most likely, were using techniques which were designed to prepare children for living under a dictator, in a society which was much more authoritarian than today's society here in North America.

To function well in a democratic society we need to be responsible as opposed to obedient and assertive as opposed to submissive. This demand for assertiveness is often difficult for us to meet because our childhood training did not include parenting techniques that developed our assertiveness.

To develop our assertiveness skills we not only need a clear understanding of what assertiveness is, we also need to revise our thoughts, feelings and the non-verbal messages we communicate to others. It is these messages which inform others that we can be easily intimidated. Consider the twelve following points:

## 12 GUIDELINES FOR ASSERTIVENESS

### 1. BEING KIND AND FIRM

Assertiveness is not being passive, aggressive or superior. It is a balanced combination of respecting the other person (being kind) and respecting yourself (being firm).

### 2. UNDERESTIMATING

We have been trained to overestimate what others should do and underestimate what we can do. Example:

We were about to present a workshop to a group of about 100 people. The majority of these people had brought their children along to play in the next room. Unfortunately, there was no door between the two rooms. We were standing at one end of the room and the audience was sitting at the other end. We asked the audience to move in closer to combat the noise from all the children in the next room. No one moved. We asked again with still no response. By this time we were both feeling a little aggravated. We thought to ourselves, *"We traveled a thousand miles to speak to this group and they don't have enough consideration to move a few feet closer so that they can hear us!"* Finally, one of us suggested, *"Why don't we just move closer to them?!"*

Easy solution, right? Why did we go through all that mental anguish trying to move 100 people who didn't want to move, when it was so easy to move the two of us? Because, like many of us, we have been trained to think only about what the other person should do and overlook what we can do. Here's another example:

A woman was angry at her husband because he wouldn't help with the dishes. They both worked full-time jobs and he had agreed that he would help with the household chores. But, he never did. We suggested to the woman that she concentrate on what she could do rather than to try to force her husband to do the dishes. After a few moments of thought she came to the conclusion that she would only do the dishes every other time. (Notice she said *"every other time,"* not *"every other night."*) That meant she would only do the dishes once after he did them once. If he wanted to wait a couple of nights before he did the dishes, that was fine with her. Here is how she approached her husband.

She said *"John, I've noticed that I've been complaining a lot about you not doing the dishes. I imagine that it feels lousy to you to hear me complaining all the time and I don't like myself when I complain. I've recognized that it's my fault because I frequently do more than my share and then I put you down. So, from now on I'll only do the dishes every other time. Then I won't make you so mad by complaining."* Much to her surprise her husband said, *"Why don't we do the dishes together?"*

## 3. NON ASSERTIVE THOUGHTS

We can become more assertive by recognizing how often we entertain non assertive thoughts such as:

*"If he really cared, he would know what I want."*

*"If I put up with it long enough, the problem will go away."*

*"If I stand up for my rights, others may get angry and I can't stand that."*

*"I don't deserve to have what I want."*

*"They think that I don't deserve to have what I want."*

*"I'm a better person because I gave in."*

*"Others won't give me what I want unless I get angry."*

*"If I do all the right things and if I am good, then I'll get what I want."*

## 4. TO WANT WHAT YOU WANT

You don't need to excuse or defend your preferences. You have a right to want what you want. Example:

Joan got a call from her neighbor asking her to baby-sit for her neighbor's two-year-old son. Joan really didn't want to baby-sit that day. But, she didn't have a good excuse for saying no, so Joan agreed. She resented the time she was baby-sitting. As a result, she felt cool and distant toward her neighbor.

We don't need an excuse to do the things we want. We have a right to want what we want and we have an obligation to let others know what we want and don't want. If we don't let them know, we are causing them to impose upon us unintentionally. Joan had a right to say to her neighbor, *"I don't want to baby-sit today."* The neighbor would then be free to either say *"OK"* or to further convince Joan.

## 5. WHAT WILL YOU DO?

Let the other person know what you will do. Example:

We were counseling a mother and her fourteen-year-old son. He was flunking school because he was not doing his homework. However, we knew that he did not want to be sent to another school. He was being very resistant in the session. We asked him what he wanted to gain from the session. He said, *"Nothing. I'd rather be outside goofing off."* We said that we did not want him to be in the session unless he wanted to improve on something. He got up and started to walk to the door. We stopped him and said, *"You can leave if you want to. But if you do we will call the school and tell them you have decided that you don't want to work on improving your grades. We won't force you to stay but we're unwilling to allow the school to think we are helping you while you are refusing to be helped."*

He thought for a moment and then sat down. We had one of our most effective sessions with him. We told him what WE would do, not what he had to do.

## 6. PROTECT YOURSELF

Often we don't protect ourselves even though we recognize a familiar situation that has been expensive to us in the past. Example:

You have asked your friend to stop a certain behavior. She agrees to stop, but she has agreed in the past and then broken her promise. At this point you could say, *"Thanks. That will really help. What should I do if you forget?"*

## 7. DON'T INTIMIDATE ME

Our body posture, tone of voice, the look in our eyes and our movements all work in concert to communicate to others, telling them how we expect them to treat us.

133

Hesitation sometimes communicates the message, *"Intimidate me."*

Dave walked cautiously into the boss' office and said, *"Ah... Mr. Smith?... Ah... I'd like to talk to you about getting a raise."*

Dave communicated to his boss that he was willing to be intimidated and that's exactly what happened.

## 8. DON'T MAKE THEM DEFENSIVE

Avoid making the other person feel defensive. Revise your approach (tone of voice, phrasing, etc. when the other person starts defending their behavior (explaining or being hostile).

## 9. EXPECT RESULTS

We often underestimate how our expectations influence our actions. If we don't expect to convince the other person, our uncertainty will show in our voice.

Debbie wanted to tell her husband that she was going to take a class at night school. She expected that he would put her down and intimidate her into not going. We had her role play the situation. She cautiously said, *"Ron, I think I'm going to take a class at night school..."* Then she waited for his response. Her pause was like telling him that she expected a negative reaction.

We helped her to change her expectations. She reported back that she told Ron, *"I've decided to take a class at night school. I'm so excited that I can't wait."* Her husband responded by saying, *"Good idea!"*

## 10. LOOK FOR ALTERNATIVES

Seeing only a limited number of alternatives usually indicates that we are unaware of our real intentions to avoid what is necessary to be assertive.

It may also mean that we feel unprepared to do what is needed in the situation. Since we feel unprepared we overlook it as an alternative. For example:

Larry was going to attend a conference and forgot to make hotel reservations until after the deadline had expired. He felt, *"It's too late. I won't be able to attend the conference."* He saw only one alternative. He overlooked the possibility of calling the conference center and asking for their suggestions because he felt unprepared to handle the possibility of embarrassment for not being organized enough to meet the deadline.

Whenever you see only a few alternatives, ask yourself, *"What might I be avoiding?"*

## 11. POSTPONING DECISIONS

When making a decision, be aware that postponing the decision sometimes gives control of your life to chance. This is assertive behavior only when you consciously prefer leaving things to chance. You may want to consider if your decision is being made from courage or discouragement.

## 12. I WANT

When we don't feel good about asking for what we want openly, we pursue it indirectly which is usually less effective.

## BEING NON-ASSERTIVE

Being non-assertive with little things adds to your feelings of powerlessness. The following are non-assertive methods we all sometimes use to try to get what we want. They usually aren't effective and they often disturb the relationship. Also listed are assertive alternatives.

## COMING HOME LATE

CRYING: You use *"water power"* to make the other person feel bad, hoping that they will give in or apologize. Example: *"Boo Hoo, you're late."*

SILENT TREATMENT: When she comes home late you are sad and quiet. You avoid initiating conversation and answer questions quietly with a minimum of words. Your posture says, *"Look what you've done to me."* Your motive is, *"I might not be able to get what I want but at least I can get even."*

TEMPER TANTRUMS: When he comes home late you call him names, throw things, stomp out of the house and slam the door. You are trying to scare the other person into giving you what you want. (The intimidation can sometimes take a more subtle form, like the husband who says, *"nothings wrong!"* but he silently paces the floor punching his fist into his hand.)

GUILT: In a weak tone of voice you make comparisons and talk about *"duty"*. Example: *"Judy's husband is never late."*

MORAL SUPERIORITY: You make statements which point out that you are a better person. *"I'm always home on time, I don't see why you can't be."*

ASSERTIVE ALTERNATIVE: *"I would like you to call me if you can't be home on time. Would you be willing to that?"*

## BUSINESS TRIP

MARTYR :Statements to induce guilt feelings in another person when they have asked for what they want. Hopefully, the other person will realize how much you sacrifice and will give you what you want without having to ask. Of course, you hardly ever accept the thing you wanted even when it is offered. Example: *"Yes, you can have the money for the business trip, we'll just have to get by without the new furniture that I was going to buy next week."*

ASSERTIVE ALTERNATIVE: *"I know this trip is important to you, but I have been looking forward to buying new furniture for a long time. How could we work it out so that we could do both?"*

## GOING TO A MOVIE

TESTING: Phrases or behavior that say, *"If you really loved me you would do it my way."* Example: *"You really don't want to go to the movie with me, do you?"*

*ASSERTIVE ALTERNATIVE: "Would you like to go to the movie with me? I would enjoy being with you."*

## GOING TO THE PARTY

BEGGING: Phrases that say, *"I'll do anything you want so that you'll be pleased with me."* Example: *"Please go to the party with me. I promise I won't talk business."* Usually these pleas are just good intentions. To get what you want, you may tend to make promises you don't want to keep.

THOSE GRAPES ARE SOUR ANYWAY: When you don't get what you want, you may try to numb yourself to the pain by claiming that you don't care. Example: *"I really didn't want to go to that party anyway. I've made other plans."*

I'LL SHOW YOU IT DOESN'T BOTHER ME: When you don't get what you want, you try to hurt the other person by saying they don't affect you. The problem with this method is that the consequences are often more painful to you than to the person you were trying to hurt.

ASSERTIVE ALTERNATIVE: *"It hurts to hear you say that you don't want to go to the party with me. What can I do to make you feel more like going with me?"*

## IT'S YOUR FAULT

BLAMING: Statements designed to make the other person feel so bad about herself that she'll give in. Example: *"It was your wise idea in the first place. If it weren't for you, we wouldn't be in this mess."*

ASSERTIVE ALTERNATIVE: *"What can we to change the predicament we are in?"*

## I WANT A DISHWASHER

COMPLAINING: *"I don't see why we can't get a new dishwasher. This one leaks all over the kitchen. Besides, it's probably rusted out and it sounds like a train when it's running."*

One reason for complaining is that if we don't feel we have a right to want something, we sometimes justify asking for it by exaggerating its importance. It is as if the person in the above example is saying, *"I don't really want something for me. It's just that the dishwasher is falling apart!"* She uses an angry tone of voice as a distraction so that the other person doesn't question what she feels is selfish. She doesn't recognize that she has a right to ask openly for a new dishwasher.

Another reason for complaining is we often don't like to take responsibility for the outcome of the decisions we make. By exaggerating the *"need"* for a new dishwasher, she is attempting to convince her spouse to take the responsibility for making the decision.

ASSERTIVE ALTERNATIVE: *"I would like a new dishwasher. Let's go buy one tomorrow."*

## DANCING TOO CLOSE

THREATENING: This tactic is used to scare the other person into doing it your way. Example: *"If you ever dance that close with another man again, I'm leaving you!"*

*ASSERTIVE ALTERNATIVE: "I feel unwanted when you dance that close to him. I don't want you to do that again."*

## GETTING A RAISE

Compare these two examples of Sue asking for a raise.

Example #1:

| | |
|---|---|
| Sue | *"Ah, excuse me. I know you're awfully busy but I've got something I need to talk to you about. It'll take only a few minutes."* |
| Employer: | *"What is it, Sue?"* |
| Sue: | *"Well, ah, I have been working here for three years now and I've really    worked hard. There have been a few times that I've come in late but usually I'm on    time."* |
| Employer: | *"Yes, Susan. Was there something you wanted?"* |
| Sue | *"Well, do you think you could give me a raise?"* |

139

Employer:     *"I would like to Sue, but I just can't at this time."*

Sue:     *"Oh... Okay."*

Example #2:

Sue:     *"Do you have 10 minutes. I would like to talk with you?"*

Employer:     *"Sure, come on in."*

Sue:     *"I would like to get a raise."*

Employer:     *"Well, I don't think that's possible right now. Money's pretty tight."*

Sue:     *"What would I have to do to get a raise in three months?"*

Employer:     *"Well, I don't know. I really can't afford it."*

Sue:     *"What if I was able to raise my sales by 5% each month?"*

Employer:     *"That would be great."*

Sue:     *"How much of a raise would you be willing to give me if I achieved that goal?"*

Notice how in this last example Sue's employer does not get imposed upon by Sue's assertiveness. Sue found a way in which both she and her employer could win.

Assertiveness is not getting the other guy to give in to what you want. It is finding a way that you both benefit from your cooperative efforts.

Many people misinterpret being assertive as being aggressive.

In the first example, Sue was extremely humble and apologized for herself several times. She was giving the message that what she had to say wasn't important.

Also, in the first example Sue *"beat around the bush"* about what she wanted. It was as if she had to defend or justify her reasons for wanting a raise. In the second example, Sue was very direct and clear about what she wanted.

Phrases like *"do you think,"* used in the first example put much of the power in the hands of the employer. This leaves Sue open for intimidation.

In the second example, Sue didn't stop at the first sign of a negative response from the employer. She continued to try to get what she wanted in an assertive way. It is difficult to think of creative solutions to a problem if you are feeling paralyzed by intimidation.

## THE ART OF CONFLICT SOLVING

It is possible that the ability to solve conflicts is one of the most valuable assets a person can possess. However, few of us have received any formal training in the art of conflict solving. We, therefore, often find ourselves the victim of someone else's desires or of an aggressor who desperately tries to maintain more power and control than others. We must develop our skills of cooperation and learn to make arrangements where both parties can win. Only then can we realize the satisfaction of intimacy and teamwork.

The following is a list of considerations you can use as tools to find new solutions to conflict situations. The suggestions are grouped to apply to different stages of the conflict solving process. We give points to think about before you start talking, things to consider in planning what you will talk about, things to avoid saying and some hints to guide you when you're thinking about a conflict or talking about it with others.

Before you go on, place in mind a conflict that you can remember clearly. Relate the following suggestions to your personal situation.

## BEFORE YOU TALK

1.  Start thinking about your part of the conflict. It is easier to change what you do than to change the other person.

2.  Recognize that no one is a victim. All problems are cooperative. Hostile feelings are usually to disguise what YOU can do about the situation.

3.  To help identify your investment in the conflict ask yourself, *"What is life demanding of me that I don't want to do?"*

Perhaps:

>   I don't want to create a hassle.
>   I don't want to have my shortcomings revealed.
>   I don't want to give up doing it my way.
>   I don't want to admit that I made a mistake.
>   I don't want to be ignored.
>   I don't want to risk being rejected.

4.  Ask yourself if you are making excessive demands.

Perhaps:

>   I wanted to be treated specially.
>   I want something for nothing.
>   I want to do it my way.
>   I want others to feel sorry for me.
>   I want to prove that I'm better than the others.
>   I want someone to do it for me.
>   I want someone else to take the blame.
>   I want someone to spend time arguing with me.

I want the other person to suffer.
I want it to look like I'm being held back.
I want an excuse for some upcoming test.
I want to discourage the other person.
I want more excitement
I want my friends to be perfect.
What I really want to say is, *"No."*

5.  Ask yourself: *"Why might I want distance in our relationship right now?"*

    *What might I be discouraged about?*

    *Am I underestimating my ability to get what I want without being angry?*

6.  Does the other person feel that I don't respect him? If you don't respect the person it will come across in your tone of voice or the words you choose. You don't need to respect everything about him but you do need to portray a genuine respect for him as a person.

7.  If the other person were to refuse to do anything about the problem, what could I do about the problem?

8.  Refrain from acting on first impulse. Sidestep the power struggle. If you buy into the power struggle, the conflict will only escalate. You may want to tell the other person that you don't want to get angry because your relationship is important to you. You're going to go for a walk or go into the next room to cool off. You'll come back and talk about it later. Make sure you don't slam the door on the way out!

9.  You can sometimes decide to stop fighting without finding the reason for the fight.

10.     Some problems can be tolerated. Is it really that important that he forgets to put the cap on the toothpaste? Is the issue more valuable than the friendship?

## TALKING

1.      Start by discussing what YOU may be doing wrong. *"I've noticed that I've been nagging you lately. I'll bet that's been making you feel lousy."* Or, *"I guess I'm feeling discouraged right now and maybe what I'm going to say is just a put-down. Will you let me know if it starts sounding like that?"*

2.      Watch your tone of voice.

3.      If you are feeling attacked, recognize that the other person is probably feeling discouraged and could be attempting to protect himself. Do not take it personally. Instead, make him feel wanted. This is difficult to do but it will expedite the resolution.

4.      If the other person starts feeling accused (defending himself, explaining his behavior, or retorting with something hostile), back off. Recognize that he probably interpreted what you have said as if you were accusing him for your problem. Start talking about what you did wrong.

Example:

Bob:     *"I don't understand why you have to always bring so much work home with you every night! We can never do anything fun."*

Nancy:   *"Look, my work is very important to me. Besides, you spend most of your evenings buried in the newspaper. I don't see what the big deal is."*

Bob:  *"Sounds like I made you angry. I guess that I'm so tired after work that I don't really feel like doing anything. I was blaming you instead of looking at what I was doing."*

Nancy:  *"That's OK. I do the same thing. Maybe we could plan one night during the week where we play tennis, racket ball, or go out to dinner."*

Bob:  *"That's a great idea. How about Wednesdays?*

5.  Take responsibility not only for what you said, but also for how the other person interpreted what you said.  *"Did you feel put down with what I just said?"*

Some people believe that once they have said something, they are no longer responsible. i.e.., *"I can't help it if she took it that way!"*

6.  Sometimes it is helpful to think about things you like about the other person before you talk.  This will help minimize your own hostile feelings and it will improve your tone of voice.

When someone does something that we are angry about, we tend to strike back.  If instead, you think about something you like about him, it places the emphasis on the importance of your relationship.  It establishes a problem solving atmosphere as opposed to distancing the relationship.

If you find that you can't think of anything you respect or like about that person, then recognize that you want to maintain the conflict.

7.  Paraphrase the other person's problem as you think you heard it.  When we're angry, we sometimes interpret things incorrectly.  Paraphrasing helps alleviate faulty interpretations.  It also shows the other person that you are listening and interested.

It communicates that his concern about the conflict is just as important as yours. However, this is not enough. You must listen AND take corrective action.

8.    It is often helpful to objectively state what you see the other person doing. This can help the other person to recognize how she is being interpreted. Example: *"You look like you're feeling angry."* Or *"When I said... it looked like that made you feel bad."* The purpose is not to get a confession, but to open lines of communication. If the person denies having those feelings, you may want to ask, *"What were you feeling?"* or you may want to drop the subject.

9.    Put yourself in the other person's place (empathize). *"If I were you, I'd be angry too."* Make sure this is sincere. People can tell when they are being manipulated.

10.   If you catch yourself putting the other person down, blaming, defending, name calling, etc. that is usually a good indication that you, for some reason, don't want to stop the conflict. You can then ask yourself, *"Why might I want the conflict to continue?"*

11.   Ask yourself: *"What do I really want: Do I want distance right now or do I want to be close?"* Frequently we fool ourselves by thinking that we want to resolve the conflict when actually we want to get even, intimidate or create a distraction.

12.   Ask the other person what they think YOU should do about the problem. (Watch your tone of voice so that it doesn't imply that you feel that the other person is responsible for causing the conflict.) Say, *"What would you suggest that I should do about....?"* Avoid saying, *"What are YOU going to do about....?"*

13.     Ask questions that lead to promoting agreement. *"What are the reasons why you want it this way?" "What would happen if we...?" "Should we try... for a while and see if it helps?"* You may want to brainstorm, write down all the alternatives, and then choose the one you both can agree on.

14.     Tell the other person why you are willing or unwilling to do what he suggests. Be kind and firm at the same time. Explain the purposes of your preferences.

15.     Tell the other person what you would like him to do. Ask if 'he is willing to do it. If he says yes and you aren't sure if he will follow through, ask him what you should do if he doesn't follow through.

16.     Be selfish, ask for what you want. Don't try to change something because it would be good for them. *"I think we should leave now because you have to get up early tomorrow."* versus *"I would like to leave now."*

17.     Don't agree to do anything you are unwilling to do, unless you want to extend the conflict.

18.     You don't have to solve the entire problem. You can just work for an improvement of the situation.

## THINGS TO AVOID SAYING

1.      Don't talk about what THEY should have done, but tell them what YOU would like them to do or what you will do.

2.      Don't defend or you will destroy mutual respect by putting yourself in a one-down position.

3.    Don't waste energy discussing a complaint unless you're certain the complaint is the real problem. The real problem is seldom money, sex, or the kids. But more likely:

Who's in control?
Who's better than who?
Who isn't doing their share?
Who might get rejected? etc.

4.    Don't complain about the past. Ask for what you want in the future.

5.    If you recognize that you want to get even, say so directly. *"I guess I still feel like hurting you back."* It makes it amazingly difficult to still feel like hurting when it's out in the open.

6.    Avoid name calling.

7.    Avoid exaggerations like *"you always"* or *"you never."*

8.    Avoid threats like, *"I don't know if I'll ever be able to trust you again."* or *"If you ever do that to me again I'm leaving."* If you do tell the other person how you will respond to their future behavior, tell them only to inform them, not to manipulate them.

9.    Refrain from talking when the other person seems to feel hurt by your words. Otherwise your words will be used as ammunition to maintain the battle.

10.    Don't give advice or criticism without first asking for permission. For example: *"May I tell you about something you do that bothers me?"*

## THINKING AND TALKING ABOUT OTHERS

1.    When you catch yourself having hostile feelings, putting the other person down, or talking

148

unfavorably about them behind their back, realize that you are discouraging yourself. Why not put that energy into something more constructive? Think about what you could do to make your life nicer. Do this every time you catch yourself wasting time thinking about their humanness.

2.      Avoid comparing unless you want to discourage yourself. When your comparison shows that you are better than others, you rob yourself of your freedom to make mistakes. When your comparisons show you aren't as good as others, you are more likely to feel like giving up.

## HOW IT LOOKS

Let's take a look at how one issue can either succeed or fail depending on the methods of conflict solving used.

Example #1:

Mary:      *"I suppose you don't want to go with me to my office party, do you?"*

John:      *"I always get so bored there."*

Mary:      *"Well, thanks a lot. You aren't the most exciting person to be with either. I went with you to your office party last month. I was bored to tears, but I didn't make a big issue of it."*

John:      *"My friends at least talk about more exciting things than real estate all evening."*

Mary:      *"Well, if you don't like my friends, I'll just go to the party alone. You can just forget about me going with you to any more of your office parties."*

Example # 2:

Mary:     *"Will you come with me to my office party?"*

John:     *"It's always so boring at those parties."*

Mary:     *"I know that they're my friends and we do talk a lot about real estate. But I would really like to be with you tonight. What could I do to make you feel like coming along?"*

John:     *"Well, I'll be willing to go for an hour. If I'm still bored, then I would like to go home."*

Mary:     *"Okay, that sounds fair to me. Thanks."*

Let's look at the steps Mary used to successfully solve the conflict.

1. Mary asked assertively for what she wanted.

In the first example, Mary's initial request was testing and set the expectation that John wouldn't go with her.

2. Mary didn't take John's comment about being bored personally. She didn't dig up the past to make him feel bad enough to change his mind. She concentrated on reaching mutual agreement on the issue.

3. Mary empathized with how John might be feeling rather than attacking back. Promoting agreement was again more important to her than hurting John back.

4. She emphasized that she wanted to be with him, to make him feel important.

5. Mary assumed the responsibility for making the evening work out for both of them by asking if there was anything she could do to make him feel like coming along.

6. She showed appreciation for his willingness to come to an agreement.

## DON'T GET EVEN, GET WHAT YOU WANT

Sometimes we don't want to resolve the conflict. We only want to hurt the other person the way we feel hurt.

In our classes for parents we do an experiential technique originated by John Taylor Ph.D. from Salem, Oregon which has a surprise conclusion. We divide the people into two groups, the A's and the B's. The A's stand on a chair and the B's kneel at the foot of the chair looking up. We explain to the A's that we want the B's to feel what it is like to be a small child. We ask the A's to shake their finger at the B's and scold them in a loud voice. The A's do as we ask but the have a difficult time acting mad. They usually laugh and smile while quietly scolding the B's. Then we instruct them to do several other things to the B's such as pat them on the head and talk to them in baby talk, pull on their arms and say, *"Let's go shopping."*

We then have the A's and B's switch positions and guess what? The B's have no difficulty whatsoever in getting angry. They yell at the A's.

In less than two minutes, the A's have created in the B's, feelings of revenge and the desire for hostile retaliation. This was accomplished by just doing one thing. They made the B's aware of how powerless they WERE!

This reaction happens with children and adults. Making the person feel powerless develops feelings of revenge.

Think about a time in your life, either as a child or as an adult, when you were overpowered by someone. What did you feel like doing if you could get away with it? Did you feel like calling him obscene names, striking back physically, or humiliating him in front of his friends, etc.?

151

## REVENGE? ME?

We would cause ourselves less trouble if we became aware of our desires to get even. However, in order to maintain both social acceptance (people who are revengeful risk loss of social status) and keep our self-concept intact (it is difficult to maintain a high opinion of ourselves if we are aware that we are using our energy to hurt others) we usually choose to be unaware of our desire for revenge. If we knew that we were trying to get even we could not maintain a clear conscience.

We do not use our conscience to prevent *"misbehavior"*. We use it to make ourselves feel like we are well-behaved. If we were ever to actually utilize our conscience as something other than an alibi, it would prevent us from *"misbehaving"*.

Unfortunately we rarely do this. Instead we all usually use unawareness.

## UNAWARENESS

Just as the person who is making you feel powerless is unaware of what they are doing to you, you also, avoid becoming aware of what you are doing to others. The fact is that we are seldom aware of our REAL intentions. We almost always see ourselves as if we only mean well, even at times when we are acting to serve the most selfish intentions.

This ability to be unaware of our own mischief allows us to perform the antisocial act, while keeping a clear conscience. We suffer the consequences of the actual mischief. We also, in the process of trying to prove that we are not responsible, create additional problems for ourselves. Example:

## THE POINT OF NO RETURN

Sixteen-year-old Susan was pregnant. When asked why she and her boyfriend, Tom, did not bother to use any form of birth control she said, *"We never meant to go all the way. We were just sitting in the car and kissing. One thing led to another. The next thing we knew we were beyond the point of no return."*

Susan's claim of good intentions will not alleviate her pregnancy. Their unawareness created additional problems In fact, if she and Tom would have had the courage to be aware of their intentions to have intercourse they could have at least taken precautions to avoid the pregnancy. But how could they have done anything to prepare for intercourse and still have claimed that they didn't intend to do anything?

If they had decided to be aware of their intentions they may have reconsidered being sexually involved. They would have realized that they were sacrificing the feeling of self esteem for expedient gratification. Instead they proceeded, innocent of their intentions, blaming the resulting problems on their physical limitations. They claimed that they didn't intend to *"go all the way"* but they went beyond *"the point of no return."*

Does such a point really exist? What if Tom and Susan were on the sofa in her home? They started innocently kissing. One thing leads to another and all of a sudden they go *"beyond the point of no return"* Just then Susan's parents walk in. Do you think Tom and Susan would be unable to stop and would continue their sexual activities for another fifteen minutes? That would be the case if there were really a *"point of no return."* Is this *"point of no return"* only in force when it is convenient?

## WHERE YOU DENY POWER

Where, in your life, are you claiming to be beyond the point of no return? Where are you denying your power and responsibility in the situation? Do you ever use any of the following phrases? If so, consider the definition following each phrase.

*"I'm sorry, I really didn't mean to..."*

DEFINITION: *"I don't intend to do anything to make it up to you, but please don't get even."*

*"I couldn't help it."*

DEFINITION *"I didn't want to do what I did, but I was not able to control my body and my body did things that I didn't want it to do. So don't blame me."*

*"What I really meant to say was...."*

DEFINITION *"My tongue isn't connected to my brain."*

*"Sorry, I just can't make it."*

DEFINITION: *"I want to come but something else is controlling me and I am not allowed to make my own decisions."*

*"I need to go now"*

DEFINITION: *"I want to stay but if I don't leave now I will die."*

*"I couldn't control myself."*

DEFINITION: *"I'm really two people. Me, and myself. Me is the one that I really am, and me is good and always wants to do the right thing. However, myself is bigger than me and is very hard to control. Myself is the bad guy, so if anything is wrong, see him, and leave me alone."*

*"The devil made me do it."*

DEFINITION: *"Evil forces control my life."*

154

*"I want to, but...."*

DEFINITION *of the word, BUT: "Forget everything I've said so far, here comes the real truth."*

*"I intended to..."*

DEFINITION: *"Judge me on my intentions, not on my actions."*

*"Things just got out of hand."*

DEFINITION: *"If my grip was stronger I would never do anything wrong."*

Notice that each of the above phrases claim good intentions that are stifled by some power beyond the individual's control. In each case, the person was not being responsible for what he did or said. How would you be seen by others if you replaced the above phrases with the following?

Instead of saying: *"I'm sorry..."*
Say, *"I didn't take you into consideration when I did that. What would you like me to do to make it up to you?"*

Instead of saying: *"I couldn't help it."*
Say, *"I didn't do enough to prevent it."*

Instead of saying: *"What I really meant to say was...."*
Say, *"I didn't make myself clear."*

Instead of saying: *"Sorry, I just can't make it."*
Say, *"I won't be coming."*

Instead of saying: *"I need to go now"*
Say, *"I want to go now."*

Instead of saying: *"I couldn't control myself."*
Say, *"I may have done the wrong thing."*

Instead of saying: *"The devil made me do it."*

Say, *"Yes, I did it."*

Instead of saying: *"I want to, but...."*
Say, *"I'm unwilling to... "*

Instead of saying: *"I intended to..."*
Say, *"I made a mistake. I agreed to do something I didn't want to do."*

Instead of saying: *"Things just got out of hand."*
Say, *"I didn't do a good enough job of keeping things in control."*

Notice that each of these revised phrases communicates an image of responsibility, confidence, strength and a willingness to pay for your own errors.

Since we are the ones who will pay the price for our own mistakes regardless of what the other person thinks, why not face our errors in a way that communicates self-reliance and accountability?

## RECOGNIZING OUR MISCHIEF

There is another benefit of using these responsible phrases. When we have the courage to admit that we are wrong, we become more willing to recognize our subconscious mischief.

Try asking yourself, *"I wonder if I'm trying to improve the situation or am I just trying to get even?"* If, after asking that question, you feel a strong desire to prove that you are not trying to get even, then you probably ARE intending revenge. Try taking responsibility for the results you achieve as opposed to claiming good intentions. Say to yourself, *"It will be interesting to see if I make the other person feel like co-operating with me or like hurting me."* Then, watch their response to see how they are interpreting what you are saying or doing. See if they are feeling closer to you or if they are feeling hurt. Then, by your results, you will know what you were up to. For example:

One day Jack and Sue were sitting in their living room and Sue said, *"Wouldn't that be fun?"*

Jack sarcastically responded, *"Oh sure, that would be great fun. What on earth are you talking about?"* Later, after she had explained what she was talking about Jack was tempted to talk to her about her error. He was going to say, *"Sue, do you realize that you only said half a sentence? You are a professional businesswoman and you can't even complete a sentence. You're going to have to improve that."*

Before he said it he decided to ask himself, *"I wonder if I am trying to help Sue improve or if I'm trying to hurt her?"* he thought, *"It will be interesting to see if what I say will make her angry or help her to become a better executive."*

Suddenly, after accepting responsibility for the results, he noticed that he was giving much more consideration to what he was about to say. *"Maybe I should first ask her if she wants a suggestion....no, that wouldn't work. Perhaps I should say that I have noticed something that she should improve on...no, that might just make her feel defensive."* His thinking process was directed more toward how she would respond as opposed to earlier when he was thinking only about what she had done wrong. Finally after much thought he decided his best approach would be to start by talking about what he was doing wrong. That would set an atmosphere where it was OK to be imperfect. He said to her, *"Sue, I noticed that I was pretty sarcastic to you a few minutes ago and I was wondering if that makes you feel bad when I do things like that?"*

He was totally unprepared for her answer! It made him see the whole situation differently. She said, *"Yes it did. I used to really enjoy how the two of us always thought so much alike. We were so interested in each other that we could just say a few words. The other person would know exactly what we were talking about. It seems that lately we have stopped doing that, and I miss it."*

She was right! In fact, when she had said, *"Wouldn't that be fun?"* he did know what she had been referring to! Thanks to the fact that he took responsibility for his results, he not only was able to avoid disturbing their relationship by hurting Sue, but he also was able to learn something from her about how he was neglecting closeness.

If you take responsibility for the results you get, you will be encouraging yourself to behave more responsibly.

## DEFUSING OUR OWN REVENGE

Once we have the courage to allow ourselves to be aware of our own revenge motives we are then in a position where we can do many things to defuse our revenge.

Scott was 10 minutes late to a class he was teaching with Dawn. He had been in a counseling session with one of his clients. The client was making a lot of progress so Scott had spent an extra 10 minutes with him. Several weeks before, Scott had made an agreement with Dawn that he would not be late so that she would not have to start the parenting class alone. Yes, he had broken his agreement, but only with good reason!

Scott sat down next to Dawn and she didn't even look over at him. She started giving him the *"silent treatment."* She was obviously getting even with him. Even though he deserved it he felt hostile towards her. He wasn't thinking about how he had broken his promise. He was thinking about how rude Dawn was being to him. He responded by acting as if he was disgusted with her.

Suddenly, after about five minutes, Dawn changed. She looked over at him and smiled.

At the break she took him aside and said, *"I was really angry at you for being late, but I decided that I didn't want to disturb*

158

*our business relationship by getting even. Instead what I would like is for you to do something, either tonight or tomorrow, to make it up to me. It doesn't have to be big - just a surprise."*

Scott felt great! She was allowing him to be human and make mistakes. She still respected him and all he had to do was to make it up to her. He recognized that he felt so good toward Dawn that he was taking every opportunity to complement her.

Scott no longer remembers exactly what he did to make it up to Dawn. However, he has been using the technique ever since. It is an excellent way to defuse your feelings of revenge.

## 2 STEPS TO DEFUSE OTHER'S REVENGE

Let's assume that someone has overpowered you and you made the mistake of hurting them back or made them feel one-down. Now, recognizing your part in the mutual retaliation, you want to stop, but they don't want to. Because of all the past hurts, you still feel revengeful. Even though you're willing to give that up, you're not particularly interested in getting too intimate with them. How can you defuse their revenge and still feel satisfied about your own retaliation? How can you get your revenge without evoking further retaliation on their part?

Since sulking, suicide and giving up are generally seen by our opponents as confirmation of how right they are, and assuming that you wish to give them as little satisfaction as possible, why not try the following two-step approach .

What could possibly disappoint your enemy more than seeing you succeed personally? And what if he was given nothing from you that could be used to justify hurting you back? What would happen if every time you became aware that you were thinking hostile thoughts about him, (or worse yet, putting him down when talking to others) you asked yourself these two questions?

1. *What is one thing that I respect about that @#$%!\*!!?*

2. *What is one thing that I could do to make life a little nicer for me?*

These two steps may sound crazy, so first we will give you an example of how they have worked, then we'll explain our opinion of why they work.

Betty was a member of a club that I belonged to. She was a psychologist; however, she was trained in a type of psychology that was theoretically almost opposite to Adlerian psychology. Our views about what caused human difficulties couldn't be further apart.

Our psychological differences began to disturb our relationship. Each of us started subtly putting the other down. I didn't like her and she didn't like me.

One day, on the way to the club meeting I caught myself discussing all the faults of Betty. I realized that her hostility toward me was hurting my reputation with the other club members, (Notice that I did not recognize how much I was hurting her.) I decided to apply the two steps of defusing revenge.

I first asked myself, "What do I respect about Betty?" It seemed difficult to come up with anything at all. However, after wrestling with myself to avoid my desires to accentuate her weaknesses, I finally admitted that she was really well-learned in her type of psychology. When she discussed her cases, it was evident that she took extremely detailed notes of her sessions with clients. She was definitely a hard worker.

Then I went on to plan what I could do to become a better therapists myself. For the rest of the trip to the club meeting, I replaced my competitive thoughts with thoughts of how to improve my usefulness to my clients.

## MAGIC RESULTS

The results amazed me! Fifteen minutes after arriving at the club, Betty came over to me and started a conversation. I actually enjoyed talking to her! The following week she referred one of her clients to a class I was teaching. As time went by I began to enjoy Betty more and more. We became good friends and I even invited her to parties.

Why did this two-step procedure work? By following step one, and concentrating on what I respected about Betty, I changed my attitude toward her. Whenever we lack respect for an individual it shows. It shows in our eyes, our tone of voice and in our facial expressions. When we communicate our disrespect, it allows the other person to forget about what they have done wrong and concentrate on how rude you are being to them. It makes them want to prove that you are wrong. For example:

Suppose someone pulls out in front of you on the highway, causing you to brake to avoid hitting them. Your response may be to lay on your horn. BEEP! BEEP! BEEP! BEEP! BEEP!

What does the offender do then? Does he wave thanks to you for reminding him to drive more safely? Does he ponder his mistake, realizing that it could have cost him his life? OR does he raise a finger in a sign of contempt and swear to himself about how rude you are to make so much noise with your horn?

## OTHER-INFLICTED PAIN EXCUSES MISCHIEF

I've never been on the scene when a police officer arrests a burglar. I hope they don't actually do it the way it's done on TV. Television usually shows the officers rudely throwing the burglar onto the ground and tightening the handcuffs too tight. They seem to operate on the principle that if they hurt the other person, then the other person will learn. The opposite is true. Other-inflicted pain allows the violator to excuse his own mischief. Other-inflicted

161

pain allows the wrong doer to shift his attention away from his own wrongdoing to the inappropriate behavior of the person that is hurting him. Whereas, respecting the person, even while he is in the wrong, allows him to reconsider his own mistakes.

When we show that we do not respect a person, we actually strengthen the bond between that person and ourselves. The other person feels the need to either prove that our opinion is wrong, or prove that we are such a shabby character that our opinion doesn't matter anyway.

Therefore, shifting our thinking to respecting the other person and working on improving our own lives makes drastic improvements in disturbed relationships.

# *Chapter Six*

tm

# THE OTHER SEX

### Nine Suggestions

To have a successful relationship it is necessary to manage the quality of the time you spend together. Others have often asked, "How do you do that?" To answer we have nine suggestions:

1.  Avoid criticizing each other.

2.  Avoid blaming each other.

3.  Avoid holding grudges.

4.  Avoid worrying about not getting your fair share.

5.  Discuss differences before they become problems.

6.  Recognize your own discouragement the moment it starts.

7.    Recognize our partner's discouragement when it starts.

8.    Promote agreement when you have conflicting desires.

9.    Don't avoid being yourselves. This gives you the freedom of being alone while enjoying the satisfaction of being together.

We have given many people these suggestions and their response is usually, *"Easier said than done."* We agree. Before you can apply these nine suggestions, you must first revise the factors that have been preventing you from applying them.

## OUTLINE FOR IMPROVING RELATIONSHIPS

Many people have come to me for counseling because of problems in their love relationships. They are missing out on the satisfaction of love. The following outline explains why and shows how to improve upon the problem.

A.  Others miss out on the satisfaction of love because they either avoid relationships, or experience dissatisfaction with the relationship they do have. These two problems cause them to experience pain in the form of loneliness, conflict, lack of intimacy, or desire for distance. They often do not understand the real cause of their problems.

See the 37 symptoms listed later in this chapter.

The real causes or mistakes are:

1.    Mistaken life style convictions.

2.    Not being prepared for changes in society.

3.    Lack of cooperation skills.

These three mistakes cause them to neglect the task of finding satisfaction in love relationships and instead they tend to pursue the tasks of:

1. Proving themselves.

2. Protecting themselves.

3. Getting even for the hurt and disappointment they feel.

4. Giving up on love and numbing themselves to the pain.

To improve on these problems they must:

1. Increase their self understanding.

   a. Recognize how they're deceiving themselves.

   b. Discover their mistaken life style convictions.

   c. Recognize the mistaken purposes they are pursuing.

2. Increase their self confidence.

   a. Stop condemning themselves.

   b. Recognize their fears.

   c. Keep their commitments

   d. Take responsibility for encouraging others.

3. Accept more responsibility.

   a. Redefine love to reflect responsibility.

    b.     Recognize how they avoid responsibility.

    c.     Develop the courage to be imperfect

4.    Decide to make a commitment.

    a.     Recognize the value of commitments.

    b.     Develop the courage to risk.

    c.     Choose their partner for a more effective reason.

5.    Adapt to changes in society.

    a.     Understand social changes.

    b.     Revise their outdated attitudes.

    c.     Develop new contracts.

    d.     Work toward improving society.

They will then be able to revise the purpose for their relationship. They will choose their partner to help them:

1.    Gain companionship.

2.    Enhance their ability to be more valuable to the community.

3.    Add more richness and fullness to their lives.

4.    Experience the satisfaction of being teammates.

5.    Experience the joy of love.

These new skills will give them the freedom to:

1.    Avoid criticizing their partner.

2. Avoid blaming their partner.

3. Avoid holding a grudge.

4. Avoid worry about not getting their fair share.

5. Discuss differences before they build momentum.

6. Recognize their discouragement the moment it starts.

7. Recognize their partner's discouragement when it starts.

8. Promote agreement when they have conflicting desires.

9. Be themselves, which will give them the freedom of being alone while enjoying the satisfaction of being together.

This will lead to:

1. Closeness.

2. Intimacy.

3. Rewarding love relationships.

After reading this far in the book, we're sure you already have a new understanding of many of the components of the above outline. There are, however, certain points we will expand upon as they specifically relate to love relationships.

## I CAN'T FIND A LOVER

For various reasons many people avoid intimate relationships with the other sex. Often they don't recognize that their objective is to avoid relationships. They come to counseling saying:

*"I can't find a lover. The ones I like aren't interested in me and the ones that are crazy about me I can't stand..." "I don't want to go to singles bars..." "I met a woman I really liked this weekend, but she lives in Ohio..." "I just haven't met the right person yet." "I keep falling in love with guys that are married..." "There just aren't any available men/women out there..."*

With all the lonely people of both sexes that have come to me for counseling making these claims, I can't understand where they must all go to avoid each other! Is it really that tough to find a member of the other sex who wants companionship?

The way I help these people is to show them that their real objective is not to find a relationship, but only to make it appear as if they are trying.

Scott had been divorced for five years. During that time he had only three short relationships with women. Then he met Sandra. He fell in love with her and they dated for four months. Scott felt that he wanted to get married; however, just when he was about to propose, Sandra's old boyfriend, Ted, returned home from the Army. She broke up with Scott and married Ted.

Scott was heartbroken. Six months later he came in for counseling. He claimed that he was still so much in love with Sandra that he wasn't even interested in other women.

Scott was not the victim of Sandra's decision to marry another man. He was not failing in his attempts to establish a relationship. To the contrary, for five and a half years he had successfully avoided relationships while, at the same time, making it appear that he was trying his best. He even chose Sandra because she communicated in the beginning that she wasn't interested in a permanent relationship with him.

We asked Scott to tell us about the moment he realized that he loved Sandra. He said, *"On our first date I told her that I was divorced. She said she could never marry me because it was against her religion. We had a great time that night and I realized how much I loved her."*

His decision to fall in love was made when she announced she would never marry him! Now he uses his unfulfilled love for her as an excuse to avoid other relationships. *"I'm still in love with Sandra. I'll never find anyone like her."* Why was he not interested in companionship?

When Scott was a child, his older sister always got top grades. She always knew what was right and often made Scott feel like he was *"just a little boy."* He developed a doubt that he could ever be a *"real man"* and believed that he had to be sure he hid his assumed inadequacies from others.

He had originally decided to get married after his mother asked him, *"When are you going to get married?"* When that marriage ended in divorce, it confirmed his expectations that he was only a *"little boy"* and couldn't really do a *"man's job"* of keeping a wife happy. His best hope was to hide his inability by avoiding relationships. His divorce had convinced him that marriage was a test he couldn't pass.

Scott was not consciously aware of either his prejudice against himself or his goal to avoid relationships. It was necessary for him to "feel" as if he really wanted to find a relationship. If he had consciously been aware of his goal it would have caused him to feel the pain of his inadequacy (loneliness).

In therapy we helped Scott revise his life style. He developed the courage to be imperfect. He started to take responsibility for the results he attained instead of putting so much energy into a pretense of good intentions.

When Scott changed his opinion of himself he discovered that he was no longer hopelessly in love with Sandra. This enabled him to reestablish his interest in other women.

A short time later he reported that he saw an attractive woman at a workshop he was attending. Then he noticed that she was wearing a wedding ring. He thought to himself, *"That's interesting, I must still be avoiding relationships because I am getting interested in unavailable women."*

Notice how Scott didn't condemn himself. He looked at his behavior as if it was an adventure. Because he did not discourage himself with self-condemnation he was able to maintain the courage to start a conversation with the woman wearing the ring. He discovered that she was separated from her husband! Six months later they were married. His new attitude helped him find a more fulfilling relationship

## $1 + 2 = 0$

If you are avoiding intimacy you may be tempted to fall in love with two people at once. In this situation the laws of mathematics do not apply because in love relationships $1 + 2 = 0$. Being in love with two people at once allows you to avoid making a commitment to either one. If you are in this predicament, or if your attempts at building a satisfying relationship aren't successful, ask yourself:

Why might I want to avoid the relationship?

Am I afraid to get too close because then I'll have to give up what I want?

Is it that I might have to risk being rejected?

Could it be that I am discouraged and doubt my ability to be happy in a relationship?

Am I looking at commitment as a test that I am unable to pass?

Do I have an unrecognized fear that encourages me to hesitate?

## MY RELATIONSHIP ISN'T INTIMATE

Intimacy is the ability to trust someone enough to share your deepest concerns about yourself, others and life, knowing that the other person will use that information to strengthen your relationship. Often people complain that their relationship is not intimate enough. Usually, this is a symptom that they are avoiding intimacy. Following are several possible reasons why someone may avoid intimacy.

## 1. FEAR OF APPEARING INADEQUATE

Some people are afraid to share situations where they feel hurt, ashamed, humiliated or inadequate. They don't share their pain with anyone because they feel that they must appear strong. They have to show others that they can handle it. They feel that if anyone else ever saw that they feel pain they would lose respect. This puts pressure on the relationship in two ways. One is that they feel alone and must hide their pain, never getting assistance while the other person never gets the satisfaction of helping. Secondly, others often resent the fact that nothing bothers you. It makes them feel inadequate and they try to prove that they can annoy you and get you upset.

No matter how capable this individual is, they get tired of always being so strong and so right, because they aren't. They are just as human as everyone else.

They underestimate the closeness they could gain and the confidence they would feel if they were to stop hiding their humanness. They overlook the fact that, when you share your pain with others (unless your relationship is seriously

171

disturbed) the other person feels closer to you and wants to be with you. Then you don't feel so alone.

Allowing your partner to share your pain often gives him a feeling of relief because he sees that he is not only one that occasionally can't handle things. He feels valuable in being able to help you. Having someone to listen to you helps you feel understood, and less alone. You don't have to prove that you can carry the whole burden.

Example: JoAnn was having difficulty at work. She normally didn't share her concerns with her husband because she was worried that he would think less of her if he knew she was having problems. In spite of her reluctance, she decided to discuss the issue with him. Much to her surprise Mike understood what she was going through. They felt warm and close to each other after the discussion. She also noticed that he started discussing more of his challenges, which gave her a chance to help him.

Sometimes this person can be very intimate, but only with certain people. There are teachers who can get close to their students, doctors who can get close to their patients, and therapists who can get close to their clients. They are only comfortable getting close where their superiority is guaranteed.

## 2. FEAR OF NOT BEING ABLE TO PROTECT THEMSELVES

Some people are afraid of not being able to protect themselves from hurt. They have allowed others to hurt them in the past and they doubt their ability to stop it from happening again. They see themselves as the victim of their partner's abuse and feel like it is out of their control. This is not true. Many of our clients who were in a position where they were getting hurt were able to do many things to prevent others from hurting them once they recognized what they gained from being the victim.

Whenever Robin and Scott had a disagreement, Scott would start yelling at her. Robin would give in and end up feeling hurt and resentful.

Prior to being adopted Robin lived in a foster home. Her foster parents comforted her frequently, whenever any of the neighborhood kids would pick on her. They did this because they felt sorry for Robin. Her biological parents had abused her and they wanted to do something to make it up to her. Robin learned to feel that, *"When someone picks on you, others will comfort and love you."* Getting abused was Robin's way of asking for love. Once she recognized this purpose she was eager to learn ways to protect herself.

During counseling, it was suggested to her that, at a time when there was not a conflict, Robin could say to Scott, *"I've noticed that when we argue, I get angry with you and feel like saying hurtful things to you. I don't want to do that. So from now on when I recognize that I'm starting to feel angry, I'm going to leave the room to cool off. I'll come back in 10 minutes to help find a solution."*

Once Robin recognized what she gained from being the victim she was able to effectively use new skills to protect herself.

Another woman reported an effective solution: when her husband raised his voice with her, she started to whisper. He had to quiet down in order to hear her.

We sometimes assume that our partner should know what hurts and not do it. It is important that you take the responsibility for telling your partner what hurts.

Example: *"It feels uncomfortable to me when you read the newspaper at the breakfast table. Would you be willing to read it at some other time? I would enjoy spending breakfast time talking with you."* (See the chapter on conflict solving for more suggestions.)

### 3. FEAR OF NOT BEING FREE

Is a person really free if he has to constantly make sure that he is never committed? The more committed a person is the deeper involved with life he is. The deeper his involvement, the more value he gets from life.

### 4. FEAR OF NOT BEING ABLE TO GET WHAT THEY WANT

Some people think it is important to put the other person first or to make sure that the other is pleased with them. They feel cautious about asking for what they want. They erroneously conclude, *"It's more comfortable to be lonely than to give up the things that I want."* They don't realize that with a few conflict solving skills, they can get what they want in a way that brings them closer to the other person.

### 37 SYMPTOMS

I often see clients for love relationship counseling who are experiencing dissatisfaction and are unaware of the real cause of their problem. Often their complaints are only the symptoms, not the cause. We examined our files and grouped these symptoms into 37 categories. Following is that list of symptoms that people complain about:

1.  I don't want a serious lover yet.

2.  I can't find a love relationship.

3.  I'm always falling in love with unavailable women.

4.  I don't want to go to singles bars, and I don't know where else I can meet someone.

5.  We're living together but can't decide if we should get married.

6. I'm in love with two people.

7. My lover just left me.

8. Since I got married my spouse has changed.

9. My marriage isn't making me happy.

10. I want more intimacy.

11. Sex isn't satisfying.

12 We have no sexual relationship.

13. My partner wants more/fewer friendships than I do.

14. We have noting in common.

15. My partner doesn't want me to get a job.

16. My partner holds me back in my job.

17. We can't communicate.

18. We fight because of the kids.

19. We fight over money.

20. The in-laws interfere.

21. I'm bored with my relationship.

22. My partner has a fault and a shortcoming.

23. My partner loses his temper, beats me, drinks, takes drugs, etc.

24. He's too busy - I want my way for a change.

25 She's become too demanding.

26. He's too chauvinistic.

27. She's too liberated.

28. I've fallen out of love.

29. I'm having an affair.

30. My partner is having an affair.

31. I'm in love with another person and can't decide if I should leave my spouse.

32. We can't decide if we should work it out or get a divorce.

33. I just got divorced.

34. My ex is interfering in my new marriage.

35. My ex is fighting with me over the kids and/or money.

36. My first wife was too bossy my second wife never speaks up.

37. ...and perhaps the most creative reason for coming to counseling was mentioned by one of our clients who admitted, *"I now realize that, at first, I only came to counseling to make it look like I was trying to solve the problem."*

When looking at the above list it appears that an insurmountable number of problems stand in the way of having an enjoyable, intimate relationship with a member of the other sex. However, if we recognize that this list is only a list of symptoms, it allows us to simplify the task of improving these difficulties. All of the above problems were solved by making an improvement in one or more of the following three basic problem areas.

## CAUSES OF INTIMACY PROBLEMS

**1.     Mistaken life style convictions.** The patterns we learned that make it difficult to be close.

For example: When Sharon was a child her parents would often say, *"Sharon, I'm disappointed in you."* Sharon interpreted this to mean that she must always be sure that others liked her. This idea became a life style conviction. In her marriage she would become paralyzed whenever the situation would require that she tell her husband that she was unhappy with something he was doing. Consequently, she put up with the situation until she was very angry. Then she would blow up, saying, *"Now that's the last straw. Why can't you ever take me into consideration?"* Eventually she withdrew from her husband because she felt it was too much of a hassle to protect herself.

**2.     Being unprepared for changes in society.** Most of us have only seen a model of love where one person is the boss and the other person is the loyal subject. To maintain intimacy we must develop ways to be together without being concerned with who is boss.

**3.     Lack of cooperation skills.** We have not had training for cooperating with people. We know how to control, please, outdo, get even, withdraw, withhold, get disgusted and make the other person wrong, but we are just beginning to learn how to be cooperators.

## MISTAKEN OBJECTIVES

When we experience one or more of the above problems it causes us to neglect the task of finding satisfaction in our love relationships and we mistakenly pursue one of the following mistaken objectives:

## 1. WE TRY TO PROVE OURSELVES

Whenever we feel inadequate we try to compensate. It becomes more important that we prove ourselves than that we enjoy intimacy.

Betsy and Steve were in a transmission repair shop. Their car had broken down and they were waiting to get the bill. Steve was showing Betsy all the parts that he recognized. *"This is a bell housing and that is a valve body. When I was younger I worked in a shop that made those parts. I designed some of the machines that make those parts."* Betsy started to feel inadequate compared to Steve and so she did nothing to acknowledge what Steve felt were great accomplishments. By the time they left the transmission repair shop they were both angry at each other.

Later, Steve was able to recognize that he was feeling unsure about his ability to be a *"good provider."* He was feeling anxious about how much it would cost to get their auto repaired. To compensate for his feeling of inadequacy he started bragging to Betsy. He had become more interested in proving himself than he was in maintaining closeness with Betsy.

## 2. WE TRY TO PROTECT OURSELVES

Occasionally we avoid relationships because we perceive them as dangerous. Our mistaken convictions cause us to attempt to protect ourselves from dangers that don't really exist.

Theresa was having trouble establishing a relationship with a man. She had started dating but broke off the relationship when he expressed a desire to kiss her passionately.

To help her recognize how she was putting too much effort into protecting herself we asked her the following questions and constructed the following chart of love's progression:

*"How would you describe the way a romantic relationship develops?"* She answered, *"First you talk, then start to trust each other, then hold hands, then hug, then kiss, then pet, then have sex, then commit to only one person, then get married."*

We then asked her, *"What would be a common-sense way to describe how most people would feel about each of the above steps?"*

Here are her answers:

## CHART OF LOVE'S PROGRESSION

| THE ACTION | COMMON SENSE |
|---|---|
| 1. Talk | Good |
| 2. Trust | Good |
| 3. Hold hands | Good |
| 4. Hug | Real good |
| 5. Kiss | Lovely |
| 6. Pet | Wonderful |
| 7. Sex | Delightful |
| 8. Commit | Secure |
| 9. Marriage | Enriching |

Then we related the chart to her actions and explained that when she started to go beyond action #5 (Kissing) she felt that she had to be cautious - she felt the need to protect herself. We then asked her to define how she felt about each of the actions on the chart. Since her feelings were often different than those listed as *"common-sense"* we could describe her feelings as being her *"private logic."* Her answers were:

| THE ACTION | COMMON SENSE | PRIVATE LOGIC |
|---|---|---|
| 1. Talk | Good | Safe |
| 2. Trust | Good | Safe |
| 3. Hold hands | Good | Safe |
| 4. Hug | Real good | Safe |
| 5. Kiss | Lovely | Careful |
| 6. Pet | Wonderful | Watch out |
| 7. Sex | Delightful | Future, future |
| 8. Commit | Secure | No thanks |
| 9. Marriage | Enriching | Don't want it |

Her actions followed her feelings. She participated in the relationship until she got to action #6. There she felt the need to retreat to action #4. When she started having that *"watch out"* feeling, she started putting distance in the relationship. Her goal was to protect herself. As counseling continued we discovered that her life style convictions were causing her to believe that getting too close to the other sex meant that she would be vulnerable to rejection. After changing her convictions she reported that she had moved in with her boyfriend. She said that she was working on getting over her fear of action #9.

### 3. WE TRY TO GET EVEN FOR THE HURT AND DISAPPOINTMENT WE FEEL.

Occasionally an individual's motive is not to get close, but to get even. Unless we have developed the courage to be imperfect, we are seldom aware of our desire for revenge. After reading Chapter 5 you already have several examples of how we all frequently use revenge, and how our unawareness prevents us from achieving satisfaction in our relationships. Getting even has disturbed many marriages and intimate relationships. To escape the vicious circle of revenge we must recognize the cycle:

1. We want something.

2. We don't get it.

3. We feel hurt.

4. We blame someone else.

5. We hurt them as we feel hurt.

6. They feel hurt by us and hurt us back.

7. Go back to step #5 and repeat cycle.

When someone is caught up in this cycle they don't go back to step #1 and improve upon their method of getting what they want. Nor do they go back to step #4 and recognize that they are holding someone else responsible for the task of making themselves happy. They just keep repeating steps # 5 and #6, escalating the pain they inflict on each other. They recognize only how they are hurt by others, and totally ignore the pain they inflict. If you are caught in this cycle, try asking yourself, *"In what ways does my partner feel hurt by me?"*

## 4. WE GIVE UP ON LOVE AND NUMB OURSELVES TO THE PAIN.

When an individual is discouraged about his chances to meet the demands of a loving, intimate relationship he may select the alternative of giving up. However, this requires that he do something to numb himself to the pain of loneliness. This is like putting clove oil on a toothache to avoid going to the dentist. If you find yourself saying things like, *"It doesn't bother me"* or *"I don't care"* then you may be trying to escape the pain of giving up. If you want to re-encourage yourself and overcome your fear you must stop resisting the pain. Ask yourself if you are really happy.

Fred came into counseling to improve some problems he was experiencing in getting along with people. He had been divorced for six years. He had dated 50 women but was close with only three of them. He had obviously given up on intimacy. We asked him if he was happy. His answer was *"yes."* He rated himself a 9.5 on a scale of 10.

We felt that he was not happy, but that he was numbing himself to the pain of loneliness. We wanted to help him recognize how much he was missing. To do this we helped him to make a graph of his life. We asked him to put five of the happiest moments of his life and five of the unhappiest moments of his life on the graph. This is the graph we helped him draw:

# HAPPINESS GRAPH

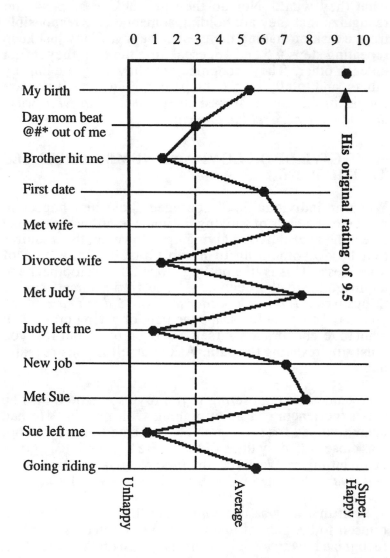

Obviously, his original rating of 9.5 on the happiness scale was nowhere near accurate. In fact, according to his own placement of his first unhappy experience, everything below a rating of 3 had to be an experience worse than having the @$*# beat out of you.

After looking at the graph he recognized that he was not happy at all. He got tears in his eyes and realized that his few happy moments were when he did have an intimate relationship with a woman.

Why was he avoiding relationships if these were the only happy moments he had? Once he stopped numbing himself to the pain he was able to use that pain to motivate himself to do what was necessary to overcome his fear.

He recognized that as a child he was always pushed aside. His parents owned a restaurant and would often say to him, *"Fred, get away from the customers!"* He felt unimportant and assumed that he had something to hide from others. Once he realized that his fears were unfounded he formed a very close and satisfying relationship with a woman.

## OVERCOMING OBSTACLES TO INTIMACY

How do we overcome these obstacles to intimacy? The first step is to increase our self understanding. To begin this process we must first recognize the excuses we give ourselves that allow us to tolerate the pain.

Dawn was describing her new boyfriend to her mother. *"Oh, Mom. I love him so much, and he's so thrifty."*

Four years later she was describing the same fellow to her divorce attorney. *"The thing I can't stand about him is that he's so cheap."*

Dawn was using her ability to assign value to a characteristic. She then fooled herself into believing that she was not biased. She uses her biased opinion to justify whatever action she decides to take. When she wants to get close she sees him as *"thrifty"* and when she wants distance he becomes *"cheap."*

As long as she does not recognize how she is deceiving herself she will never be able to see the real reason for her desire for distance. She feels that her marriage didn't work because he was cheap, when perhaps she wanted to get away because she didn't have the assertiveness skills to get what she wanted unless she was alone.

See if you can find the alibi you are using in the list of *"37 Symptoms."* If you find it there, ask yourself, *"What new skills do I need to be able to enjoy this relationship?"* Then take action. For example: If you feel that your relationship is unhappy because you fight over the kids, then take a parenting class together and discuss the suggestions so that you can come to agreement. (If you find yourself saying, *"He would never go to a parenting class with me. And even if he did he would never come to agreement."* then you know that you are very invested in blaming someone else for the problem. Ask yourself, *"In what way may it be MY fault?"*)

## FOR WHAT PURPOSE?

We can also gain insight if we explore the purpose for our choice of partners. It is not as important WHO we chose as it is WHY we chose.

Ask yourself, *"For what purpose do want this relationship?"*

## BECAUSE HAVING A RELATIONSHIP IS WHAT IS EXPECTED OF ME?

In marital counseling many people have reported situations where they decided to get married because everyone else was getting married. Some clients have disclosed: *"I was approaching age thirty and my family hassled me to get*

184

*married."* or *"We dated through high school and everyone expected us to get married."* or *"One day my mother asked me when I was going to get married."*

## TO COMPETE WITH ANOTHER MEMBER OF MY OWN SEX.

One client reported, *"My roommate was dating this guy and I thought he deserved better than that. So I started to flirt with him and eventually we got married."*

Another client reported, *"My younger brother and his girlfriend decided to get engaged. Judy and I eloped several weeks before they got married. I couldn't let my younger brother get married before me.*

## BECAUSE I WANT SOMEONE WHO WON'T COMPETE WITH ME.

You may have chosen your partner because he has opposite characteristics. For example, one person may be socially graceful, the other withdrawn and aloof. In this case the outgoing partner need not fear that her husband will challenge her title of being the most social.

## BECAUSE I WANT SOMEONE TO ADMIRE ME.

The problem with this type of relationship is the relationship goes well until the admirer gets tired of admiring.

Francie got married to a college professor. She really admired him and asked his advice whenever she ran into any personal difficulties. They had two children. After several years of being a homemaker, she decided to start her career. She completed her schooling and became a lawyer.

The more her self-confidence increased, the less she *"looked up"* to her husband, and the less she asked him for answers. She became more and more independent. Her husband became threatened and had an affair with a girl fifteen years younger than him. If he had not chosen the relationship to have someone look up to him he would not have been threatened by his wife's success.

Some individuals mistakenly feel that they must prove that they are in control. The person with that attitude may choose a partner who indicates a willingness to be controlled. The problem with this objective is that people only like being controlled when the controller's desires match their objectives. The controlled person often resorts to revenge.

Ralph was very domineering in his relationship with Jean. When Jean would attempt to assert herself, Ralph would raise his voice to intimidate her to his way of thinking. Jean did not dare challenge Ralph's control. They came into counseling because their sixteen year-old son, Nate, was always arguing with his father. Although we gave them many suggestions, the arguing continued until we recognized that Jean was getting satisfaction in seeing her husband getting defeated. When Ralph revised his need to dominate the arguments stopped and their marriage became more satisfying.

**BECAUSE I WANT SOMEONE TO TAKE CARE OF ME.**

Traditionally, most marriages were based on the man providing for and protecting the woman. The woman's role was to admire the man, support him and raise his children. Due to this, women frequently choose a marriage partner for the purpose of being taken care of because they underestimate their ability to take care of themselves. Men tend to choose a partner to take care of them when they have been pampered and confuse love with care.

## BECAUSE I WANT SOMEONE I CAN TAKE CARE OF.

It is often a worthwhile feeling to take care of someone. But the caretaker often begins complaining that she is not getting her fair share. At the same time she makes her partner feel that he is too inadequate to really help. This undermines the other person's self-confidence and keeps them dependent. For example:

Joyce had a friend who was having a hard time finding a job. So Joyce invited him to come and stay with her until he found employment. At first, Joyce felt very helpful and worthwhile by being in the position to take care of John. She rationalized his not working by the thought that they got along so well. But after several weeks she began to feel resentful for the extra burden she was allowing him to place on her. However, after she asked him to help with some of the household chores she started complaining that he didn't operate the cloths washer properly and he put the dishes on the wrong shelf.

Joyce was complaining about doing all the work while undermining John's willingness to help. Her real objective was to feel superior to John by keeping herself in the *"helper"* position.

## TO FEEL SUCCESSFUL OR FEEL PRESTIGE THROUGH YOUR MATE'S SUCCESS.

Choosing a partner to compensate for your lack of confidence in your own abilities does not solve the problem. It only increases your feelings of inadequacy.

One of the reasons Al married Marcia was because she came from a very prestigious family and she had a lot of money. After several months of marriage he recognized that he was not feeling worthwhile. He began to feel that he hadn't earned the money he was spending and wondered if he really earned the position he had in her father's company.

187

## BECAUSE I WANT SOMEONE TO PAY ATTENTION TO ME.

Angie really enjoyed Frank because he paid a lot of attention to her. He would call her several times a day and pick her up after work. When he had a special assignment at work which required that he work overtime she felt threatened and started an argument, claiming, *"You don't love me."*

The problem with choosing a mate for the purpose of having someone's attention is that you put your energy into keeping that person busy with you and neglect doing things to make your time together more enjoyable. Often times if your mate is not giving you the attention you feel you need, you go to extremes to get it. For example:

Joan's husband, Mike was being unresponsive to her requests for his attention. She felt she had tried everything civil to get him to come out from behind the newspaper. She got a glass of cold water and threw it on him. She got his attention but it pushed him further away. Next time she would have to try something even more drastic.

## TO FILL A VOID IN YOUR PERSONALITY.

Sometimes when we feel there is something lacking in our own personality, we choose a partner in an attempt to compensate for our inadequacy. For example:

Faye was shy and felt inadequate in group situations. She became attracted to Joe because he seemed confident and at ease in groups.

This arrangement can be helpful if you learn from each other and strengthen your areas of discomfort. However, the opposite frequently happens. In Faye's case, instead of learning from her husband, she compared herself to him. This only increased her awareness of her ineptness and did nothing to help her become more outgoing.

Adam was attracted to Laurie because she seemed so stable, so responsible and had a strong sense of direction. He was the opposite of those characteristics. Instead of her characteristics *"rubbing off"* on him like he had hoped, they became an area of contention in their marriage. She became resentful of how irresponsible he was. And he became disappointed in how boring and unspontaneous she was.

## BECAUSE YOU WANT SOMEONE TO HOLD YOU BACK.

Frequently, people who have high standards for themselves arrange to have something or someone to hold them back. *"I would be great if..."* or *"I would be a renowned doctor if only my wife didn't complain about how many hours I work."*

## BECAUSE HE HAS CHARACTERISTICS SIMILAR TO A PARENT OR SIBLING.

We often choose partners that will fulfill our expectations of what a relationship should be like. We tend to choose people who have characteristics that we feel familiar with. This gives us a sense of security. At least we know what to expect.

We might choose someone because he is opposite of someone we felt very uncomfortable with as a child. For example:

Karen's father was domineering. She felt that he took advantage of her mother's kindness. She married someone who was passive. However, she soon started protesting that he expected too much from her.

There are other mistaken purposes for choosing a mate that aren't listed above. You may want to explore your own reasons. The purpose of the exercise is to improve your awareness, not to dwell on the negatives. We aren't suggesting that you should find another mate. But you can choose the same mate for a different purpose. There are just as many positive reasons for your choice. If you chose for companionship, you will invite and nurture companionship. If you chose for safety, you will create distance. In chapter three we discussed how mistaken convictions of our life style leads us to pursue the wrong objectives. If you are having difficulties with the other sex, review your style from the point of, *"What did I learn to expect from the other sex?"*

We also suggest that you review how you learned about love and how to give and receive it.

## HOW YOU FELT LOVED

In our early years, each of us have devised a different answer to the question, *"What do other people have to do to prove that they love me?"* Since we answer this question based upon our childhood experiences, it is very likely we will come to mistaken conclusions. For example, a child may feel that proof of love is when the other person buys him whatever he wants.

If there was a mistake in our answer to that question, the mistake causes us to pursue mistaken objectives. To revise these errors we have found it helpful to have our clients explore their answers to the following questions.

Ask yourself:

*"How did you GET love as a child?"*

*"How did you GIVE love as a child?"*

Consider the things that you now do to try to show your love and to test the love of your partner. See if you recognize a relationship between how you act now and how you answered the questions. For example:

Marge got love as a child for working hard. Her parents had their own business. They would praise her for all the time she spent at their business working. When she didn't spend part of her weekend at the business she detected a note of subtle disapproval. As a result, she equated working with approval or love.

Even though this notion is no longer operable, Marge continued to work long hours. This became an area of contention between her husband, Mike, and her. Mike felt like Marge spent too much time working. Marge felt her efforts weren't appreciated by Mike.

Once Marge recognized the purpose of her actions, she became aware that she set herself up for working more than she should. She became aware of how she often took on more than her share. She felt she could do the work better and more efficiently than others.

She also became aware of her desire to make others notice how busy she was. She often finished one report and then ran up the stairs to bring it to her secretary. It would have been far more efficient to bring all of her reports to the secretary at one time during the day. However, others would not have seen how ambitious she was.

Another example:

Jay's wife complained that he demanded a lot from her, but that he didn't give as much as he received.

When asked how he gave love as a child Jay said, *"I was the youngest in my family. Everything was given to me without me having to do anything. When I would offer my assistance, my family would explain that they didn't need it. For instance, I offered to help Mom cook. She said that I was too small and told me to go play."*

Jay misinterpreted his early situation. He concluded that love means that others don't make demands on you. Whenever his wife would expect him to help, Jay would feel that she didn't love him.

## INCREASING SELF CONFIDENCE

To be able to get richness and fullness from a relationship with the other sex we must have the skills to develop and maintain confidence in ourselves. Following are several methods you can use to increase your self confidence:

## LIKING YOURSELF

It is difficult to believe that someone else can love you if you don't love and respect yourself. If you don't hold yourself in high esteem, you put a demand on your partner to fill your emptiness. This can lead to many difficulties in the relationship especially since the other person is usually having a hard time building his own esteem. Therefore, we suggest that you start a campaign of liking yourself so that you don't become dependent on someone else to do it for you.

Practice thinking about things that you like about yourself. Share them with the people you feel close to,

## NOT BEING YOURSELF

If an individual has a shabby opinion of himself his tendency may be to try to be something other than what he is . The following story will clarify:

## KICK THE DOG

One day, while waiting to be seated in a restaurant we were surprised to meet an old friend that Bill had known when he was in his early 20's. We invited her to join us for lunch and one of the things she told us was a shocking testimony of the futility of trying to be what you're not.

She was telling us about the time when she and Bill first met. He remembered the occasion she was referring to. It was when he was standing in her front yard talking to her and a dog came running up to her. She yelled at the dog and pushed it away with her foot.

Prior to that moment he had considered her attractive and was seriously considering dating her, but her roughness with the dog caused him to change his mind.

The shocking disclosure she made to us at the restaurant was her description of the same incident. She had said, *"I remember talking to you in my front yard. I had a crush on you. A dog came running up and I wanted to impress you so I hollered at it so that you wouldn't think that I was afraid of the dog. Afterwards I felt real sorry for the dog."*

Her efforts to make a good impression on Bill actually gave him the wrong impression! How often can you catch yourself trying to be something that you are not. It takes considerable courage to be ourselves. We could all learn from the courageous words of a counselor who was doing her internship at a mental health center.

During one of the center's team meetings she mentioned that she was in agreement with a very controversial therapy method. After the meeting her supervisor told her that she should not tell others that she agreed with that method. She asked him, *"Why not?"* He told her that if she were applying for a job as a therapist and was so open about her agreement with controversial methods she may risk not getting hired if the prospective boss didn't agree with those methods.

Her response to her supervisor was very refreshing. She said, *"If someone doesn't agree with the type of therapy that I do, then I don't want the job! I want to work for someone who appreciates me for being the person that I am. I don't want to have to pretend every day."*

Remember, no one else is like you. The world needs you, just as you are. You do not have to change. Self improvement can be a very exciting and rewarding thing, but it is not a necessity. Consider it as *"getting a little bit more out of life."* Don't look at it as something you have to do in order to become good enough.

## ENCOURAGING OURSELVES

Many people work very hard to keep themselves discouraged without being aware that they are doing it.

Carol came to counseling to get help with her depression. At many points in the counseling process she claimed that she couldn't understand. She often would announce at the start of a session, *"I still don't think I have my act together yet."*

What would happen if she would, *"get her act together?"* Why did she resist getting to the point where she could feel self confident?

When Carol was a child her mother felt very responsible for Carol's happiness. The only thing that Carol would have to do is to look a little sad and mother would go into action, doing whatever was necessary to cheer her up. Carol had learned that depression was the best tool to get what you wanted in life.

As an adult, Carol resisted feeling confident. The reason for her resistance was that, as a child, she felt that she would lose her mother's love if she were ever to say, *"Mom, I can handle things by myself now. I don't want you to do anything for me. I only want you to be with me."* She equated being confident with losing love.

Carol had concluded, as a child, that she need not take responsibility for her own happiness. Counseling helped her recognize that she was responsible for encouraging herself.

194

### FEAR UNDERMINES CONFIDENCE

Fear is perhaps the individual's biggest enemy. Perhaps the biggest joke is that we are all afraid of each other. We only recognize our own fears never the other person's.

Imagine that you are standing on a street corner and a motorcycle pulls up in front of you. The man on the cycle is wearing a black leather jacket with the sleeves cut out and a skull and crossbones painted on the back. He has long, unwashed hair, a beard and a scar on his face. His jeans are ragged and soiled and he is wearing an old German army helmet.

Would you be afraid of him? Would you lose your confidence?

Consider how hard the fellow on the cycle has worked to develop his scary image. It is as if he has a big sign on his motorcycle saying:

## PLEASE BE AFRAID OF ME!

Why does he need that sign? Perhaps he is discouraged and feels that he does not have the ability to be valuable to the community. Nevertheless he still wants to belong and believes that if he can get others to be afraid of him then others will be too intimidated to throw him out. They will be afraid to challenge his worth.

Isn't it ironic that his fear causes him to work so hard to try to scare others? The world is full of many strong people who doubt their power and make themselves appear weak by trying to prove their strength.

It is not only the fear of physical harm that threatens our self confidence. Often we fear getting too close in our relationships because we have developed a faulty self concept. We are afraid that if we ever allowed anyone to be close enough to recognize that we were not perfect, they would not accept us.

## BEING UNAWARE OF FEAR

Frequently we are unaware that we are afraid and therefore unaware of how much we allow fear to control our lives. Sometimes we don't recognize the fear because we disguise it by blaming others. Making the choice to stop blaming and taking responsibility for our own mistakes can greatly improve our self confidence.

Chuck's wife complained that Chuck would often be distant from other people. When visiting he would read a book or watch TV rather than talk with their friends. He worked many long hours and minimized his leisure time. He told his wife that he had to get his business to the point where it was self sustaining, then he could afford to settle down and spend more time with others. His relationship with his wife was often disturbed because she too felt that he seldom was really close with her.

We asked Chuck questions about his history. He told us that he had been married before. We asked him if he had any children from his previous marriage. Reluctantly he told us that he had two boys. He had not seen them since he had been divorced. We asked why and he explained that his parents had been divorced when he was a young boy. His mother always made Chuck spend weekends with his father. He felt that his mother used him to soothe his father's loneliness so that she wouldn't feel so guilty for leaving him. Chuck said he wanted to be sure that he did not make his kids feel that they had to spend their time making him happy.

We asked him if he ever missed his kids. He said *"No."* His wife said that he never wanted to talk about his previous marriage.

Chuck was blaming his mother for making him take care of his father. He was using blame to disguise his fear.

We asked Chuck, *"When was the first time you saw someone taking care of someone else?"*

Chuck's eyes welled up and he started to cry. He told us that when he was six years old his aunt got sick and came to live with them. His mother did everything for her. His aunt showed no appreciation and, from Chuck's perspective, was even mean to his mother. He remembered one time when his mother had brought his aunt her toothbrush and a pan so that she would not have to get up to brush her teeth. After using the pan to rinse her mouth, Chuck's aunt threw her toothbrush into the dirty water and Chuck's mother had to fish it out.

We helped Chuck recognize the decision he had made when he saw his aunt mistreat his mother. He had decided that he had to be afraid of getting into a position where he had to take care of someone.

His response was, *"No wonder have always hated my aunt."*

He was still blaming others and hiding his real fear.

We asked him, *"Which hurt more? Seeing your aunt being disrespectful to your mother or having your mother be so busy with your aunt that she no longer had time for you."*

Chuck broke down and cried, admitting how selfish he had felt all of his life. He said, *"I've been a real ass."*

He had finally accepted responsibility for his fears. He recognized that he was afraid that if he ever allowed anyone to get too close, they would make demands on him. When they made demands he would have to either say no, or do what they requested . He felt that taking care of someone would lead to loss of self respect, as it did with his mother. He was afraid of that. If he were to say no, it would force him to get in touch with how selfish and alone he felt. His solution to this dilemma was to avoid getting close and numb himself to how much he missed being with others.

When they came to our office for their next session Chuck looked very relaxed and confident. His wife told us that he had started making friends and had become more interested in other people. Chuck said that he had felt free to start caring for others. He had started taking on more responsibility for feeding their cat and said that caring for it had given him a feeling of satisfaction that he had never felt before. He also said that he couldn't believe how he was working fewer hours and accomplishing so much more.

Chuck was no longer feeling that he would be taken advantage of if he gave up doing something that he wanted to do in order to care for someone else. He was free to be closer to people. His comment reflected his new confidence:

*"I realized that I had no one to blame and so I just accepted that I was wrong. Doing that made me feel that I no longer had to work so hard to try to hide my selfish feelings. Now I don't feel like a terrible person, I just feel that I made a mistake. I made some calls to find where my kids are living. I'm going to see what I can do to make up for my mistake."*

## KEEPING COMMITMENTS

One of the most effective methods to build your confidence in yourself is to make and keep commitments. Every time you keep a promise you create a sense of self reliance. If you wish to make better use of this method of increasing your own self confidence it will be necessary to be aware that the decision to keep commitments can only be made at the time you make the initial promise. It is at that time that you are the most likely to agree to things that you either can't do or have no real intention of doing. At the moment you make the promise you are in the best posture to demonstrate respect for yourself. Only when the promise is being made can you take the time to plan to make sure that you can keep the agreement.

Unfortunately, most of us have been trained to blindly agree to anything in order to get what we want. We often say whatever we feel the other person wants us to say. Think about some of the insincere commitments that you have made and how you avoided keeping them:

Anna had agreed to call Jan regarding a committee meeting. Anna really didn't want to be on the committee. She felt obligated because Jan was a close friend. Anna *"forgot"* to call Jan.

Later that week Anna ran into Jan at the supermarket. She said, *"Oh, Jan. I'm sorry I didn't call you about the meeting. Things have been so hectic lately that it just slipped my mind."*

Anna damaged her self confidence. When we break an agreement, even if we hide our failure from others, we are left with the feeling that we were unable to be counted upon. While entertaining that feeling it is impossible to feel self confident.

## ACCEPTING RESPONSIBILITY

We often destroy our chances for intimacy because we avoid being responsible.

When we arrange to feel that love is beyond our control we also relinquish our ability to make our relationship what we want it to be. The desire to avoid responsibility is very evident in the way many people define love.

## DEFINITION OF LOVE

There are some popular definitions that are often used which tend to interfere with our ability to have a satisfying relationship with the other sex.

## DEFINITION #1

**Love is a hole.** It is about 40 feet deep and 3 to 4 feet in diameter. You can't see where the hole is because it is covered with something that looks like the back seat of a '57 Chivvy or the grass in the park. If you happen to step on this covering while in the presence of a member of the other sex (or occasionally, a member of your own sex), you break through the covering and fall into the hole. The sides are very slippery and no matter what you do, you can't get out. You have fallen in love.

Sometimes, for some unknown reason, this hole is upside down. Then you fall OUT of love.

## DEFINITION #2

**Love is an infection.** It is caused by the poison on the tip of an arrow that is shot by this little nude guy with wings. He is called Cupid.

Notice that both of these definitions have one thing in common. They both suggest that the individual is not responsible for his feelings of love. These definitions claim that love is beyond control. The reasons that such definitions are so popular is because we often want to avoid being responsible for the choices we make about relationships.

*"Gee, Karen, I know I should keep my promise to stay married to you, but I have fallen out of love with you and have fallen in love with Marsha."*

Karen's husband wants to break his commitment. He also wants to maintain a clear conscience and avoid being blamed for his actions. He is really saying, *"Judge me on my intentions, not on my actions. I have no control over what I do."*

The problem with this method of trying to avoid responsibility is that it doesn't work. In spite of his alibis, Karen will still get even with her husband for breaking his promise and he will still feel guilty and weaken his own self-esteem.

As a more courageous method of taking responsibility for your feelings we suggest the following new definition of love:

## NEW DEFINITION OF LOVE

*LOVE: The feelings you create after you have decided to have a close relationship with an individual. These feelings assist you in maximizing their strong points and minimizing their weak points.*

With this definition, love is a choice, not something you are forced to do because of some magical power outside yourself. Taking on full responsibility for love can even help you to find a relationship.

On one of my lecture tours, a woman came up to me and said that she had known Rudolf Dreikurs. He had come to her town seven years earlier to give a lecture and she had been assigned the job of picking him up at the airport. She explained to me how he had said a few words that had changed her life and paved the way for her to get over her fear of marriage. She said:

We were driving along talking and Dreikurs said, *"Do you mind if I ask you a personal question?"* I gave my approval and he said, *"Are you married?"* I said *"No"* and he asked, *"Why not?"* I said, *"Because I haven't fallen in love with anyone yet."* He smiled and asked, *"Do you mind if I tell you what I think?....I believe it is because you are too critical and you scare men away."* I realized that he was right and decided to stop being so critical. Three weeks later, I met my husband.

She had been excusing her faults by claiming that she had not *"fallen in love."* She was acting as if love was something that happens to you. Taking responsibility helped her to recognize her own faults. She started being more honest with herself. Her honesty allowed her to overcome the criticalness that was causing her to avoid relationships.

## BLAMING

Most people become disillusioned with their lover not because suddenly he becomes boring or unattractive. People become disillusioned with intimacy because they blame the other person for their own lack of interest. They often feel that they have chosen the wrong person and wish that they had not made a commitment. They don't need to renege on their commitment. They need to take responsibility for making their current relationship more exciting, more romantic, more spontaneous and closer.

They don't trust their own ability to decide what they want and go after it so they blame their partner. When they stop blaming and start taking action they will discover that they can make their relationship the way they want it to be. For example, if you want more romance, why not have the children gone when she comes home, have flowers on the table and nice music playing? If you want more spontaneity, why not take your husband by the hand, without telling him where you're going, place him beside you in the car, and drive to the overlook of the city night lights?

If your relationship is unhappy it is usually an indication of problems you are having with yourself. If you choose to get away from those problems by blaming and choosing another partner the problems will reappear somewhere else down the road.

It is OK to postpone dealing with your problems, but don't fool yourself by saying that your partner is to blame. It is your responsibility to be happy, feel lovable, and get what you want from life. If you expect that someone else is going to put your happiness above theirs, make you feel loved, and be able to read your mind to help you get what you want, you will continually be disillusioned. Your lover is there to support you in getting those things but not to get them for you.

## BEING IMPERFECT

We cannot realize the benefits of taking more responsibility if we do not have the courage to be imperfect. For example: If you are about to discuss a problem with your partner, say to yourself, *"It will be interesting to see if I talk about this in a way that brings us closer together or if I do it to hurt my partner."* Then you can judge yourself by the results you achieve. If your partner gets upset, you can say to yourself, *"I must have wanted to create distance in our relationship. I wonder why I feel the need for distance?"* Having the courage to accept responsibility for the results helps you learn about yourself.

## COMMITTING TO ONE PERSON

Commitment sometimes doesn't feel worth the effort it requires. It sometimes seems to be binding and cumbersome.

Ironically, making a commitment gives you freedom. Being intimate with one person, changes the way you feel about yourself and revitalizes how you feel toward life. It gives you an accepting environment where you can look at yourself and either make changes or be yourself. It gives you the feeling that someone knows almost everything there is to know about you and yet you are still accepted. This acceptance gives you extreme confidence.

Making a commitment to one person requires taking risks. Risks of being rejected, being hurt, being vulnerable. It requires work - taking the time to make sure you're understood, taking the time to do the special little thing to make your partner feel loved and wanted. It requires a willingness to put your energy into enriching the relationship you have as opposed to constantly searching for a better person.

There will always be other men or women who look like a *"better deal"*. Often we are misled to give up what we have to chase what we don't have. It is as if we were acting on the theory of, *"whatever isn't, is better than what is."* We often overlook the value of what we already have, and opt for expedient gratification.

If you find a better deal somewhere else and you decide to go to all the trouble of starting all over with a new person, what's going to keep you from searching for still another *"better deal?"*

Looking for a better deal is like being invited by friends to two different occasions at the same time, sailing or backpacking. You choose the sailing and all during that time you wonder if you made the right choice or if the party that went backpacking is having MORE fun. In the meantime, you're losing out on the fun of sailing because you haven't made a commitment to being there. Let's say you do this for several weekends in row. You'd end up feeling like why bother. I'll just stay home. Although at first it is really exciting being invited to so many occasions, after a while the excitement wears off. You end up feeling empty and alone. Think how much better you would feel if you chose one and then decided to make things happen for you.

The other part of this scenario is that when you're not committed it makes the other person feel less like making an investment in you. You lose twice. Once because you're not getting the satisfaction of what it feels like to put your all into a relationship and secondly you lose the benefits the other person brings into the relationship.

## ADAPTING TO CHANGES IN SOCIETY

In chapter four we have described many changes that have taken place in our society. Those changes also affect our ability to be intimate in our relationships with the other sex. We cannot use these changes to excuse our inability to establish a meaningful relationship. We must first understand these changes, then revise our outdated attitudes and develop new contracts that are compatible with our new social atmosphere. To gain satisfaction and feel worthwhile we must also work together to improve our society, making it a place where we are not a threat to each other.

Due to many changes in society around issues of equality between men and women, there is a lot of role confusion. It was easier for our grandparents, because they knew their roles and therefore what to expect from each other. Sometimes just realizing that we are social pioneers helps to remove pressures we feel in trying to maintain an intimate relationship. Very few of us had parents that modeled an equal relationship with mutual respect.

One of the problems that sometimes enters into our relationships is that on one hand men want women to be equal. They are tired of having to carry the burden of *"bringing home the bacon,"* making decisions, being depended on, and being the *"pillar of strength."* On the other hand, they sometimes feel threatened when a woman takes on these roles and becomes independent.

For the woman, sometimes the conflict rises when on one hand she does want to assume leadership, become independent, and be an equal contributor to the family's finances. On the other hand, women frequently have not been trained to become an equal partner. As a result, they sometimes doubt their ability.

205

## LIBERATION

Many relationships are currently threatened by the concept of liberation. Webster defines liberation as:

*...to release from slavery, enemy occupation.*

Our society puts relationships in quite a double bind. On one hand you are questioned if you aren't attached by thirty, making you dependent on the other sex for fulfillment. On the other hand, men and women frequently treat each other like enemies. I'm sure you have all been at a social function at one time or another where the men talk in one area of the room and the women in another. Or you've heard couples talk about each other as if they felt their partner was a *"pain in the neck."*

What is needed, is for both men and women to become liberated from the traditional role models and stereotypes, for both sexes not to be threatened by or doubtful of liberation. But to look at it as a challenge, an adventure. An adventure that at times will be rocky and at times we may long for the security of set roles. But in the end both sexes will feel better about themselves, each other, and their ability to work as teammates rather than enemies on a battle front.

## A NEW CONTRACT

In a democratic setting we need a new basis for relationships. In the past, dictators controlled people by promising to take care of their needs, promising security in exchange for their loyal service to the dictator. (The dictator controlled and made the decisions.) This is exemplified in the slogan, *"Yours is not to wonder why, yours is but to do or die."*

In today's democracy we must become more responsible. We must take responsibility for our own happiness rather than put demands on others to make us happy.

If we have a relationship contract that says *"I will consider your happiness more important than my own,"* we will end up being disappointed in the other person and the other person will see us as controlling. We have no way to tell, for sure, what any other person wants. When we try to second guess them, we impose upon their free will.

Instead, we suggest a contract that says, *"I won't let you hurt me. Nor will I demand that you are responsible to make me happy. I'll take responsibility for my own happiness. I'll expect the same from you."* In that way, we can both feel free enough so that our partnership does not become a burden. Then, through cooperation, we can enrich each other.

To be able to live within this type of contract it is necessary to be well trained in kind but firm assertiveness, and to have the courage to take responsibility for yourself.

## NEW FREEDOM

After applying the above principles you will have gained a new freedom. This new flexibility will now allow you to use the methods necessary to enjoy an intimate relationship. You will find that you can now:

1. Avoid criticizing each other.

2. Avoid blaming each other.

3. Avoid holding grudges.

4. Avoid worrying about not getting your fair share.

5. Discuss differences before they become problems.

6. Recognize your own discouragement the moment it starts.

7. Recognize your partner's discouragement when it starts.

8. Promote agreement when you have conflicting desires.

9. Be yourself. This gives you the freedom of being alone while enjoying the satisfaction of being together.

Following these guidelines will lead you to closeness, intimacy ad a rewarding love relationship.

## A NEW PURPOSE

You may notice that you have revised the purpose for your relationship. You may become more concerned with developing companionship, enhancing your ability to be more valuable to the community, adding more richness and fullness to your life, becoming better teammates and experiencing the joy of love.

# *Chapter Seven*

tm

# ENJOYING LIFE

### Your Reactions

At this point there are many reactions to the information presented in this book. Some people are sad. They feel like they have wasted a lot of precious time playing games.

Some people are relieved because they realize how much easier life is when they quit blaming other or excusing themselves. They realize that by taking responsibility, they feel more alive and vital.

Some people are feeling defensive. Some of you have been going through life the hard way for twenty, thirty and more years. It is understandable that you would want to defend and cherish your beliefs.

Some people are angry because they didn't want to have to face the fact that you get what you want in life, the bad along with the good. Other say, *"Yes there were some good*

*ideas, some that I didn't agree with and some that didn't
make sense for me. No big deal!"*

There are some people who feel confused. They feel lost.
One client expressed the feeling, *"I feel like the old trick
where someone pulls the table cloth from under the dishes.
However, this time they also pulled out the table.
Everything's hanging in mid air. Now that I don't want to
play those games anymore, what else can I do?"*

## BEING TOGETHER

All of the above reactions are natural because whenever
you recognize that you are following a mistaken goal in
your life it disturbs the equilibrium. It requires that you
redirect yourself to a better purpose.

The new purpose that Adler and Dreikurs recommended is
social interest. Social interest means that we live our lives
for the joy of being together, instead of striving to prove
ourselves or working to become better than others.

## WHO CARES?

Up until this time you have been spending energy making
yourself right and making others wrong, trying to control
life, trying to make others like you. You've been trying to
get other to treat you as though you are special, or trying
to avoid participating in life.

Others don't care if you're a success or a failure, if you're
rich or poor, if you're smart or dumb. They just want to be
with you! Just as in the old joke:

Fred:    *How's your wife, Bob. You two make such a
         nice couple.*

Bob:     *We're divorced.*

Fred:    *That's good. She was no good for you anyway.*

Bob probably spent many hours worrying about what his
friends would think of him because he failed in his

marriage. Fred just didn't care. He was ready to support his friend either way. He just wanted to be with Bob.

## NINE STEPS TO REDIRECT YOURSELF

What is needed now is for you to redirect your energy into things that will make your life more fulfilling and satisfying to you. Others just want to be with you, and you want only to be with them. Now that you have stopped playing all the games that didn't achieve that goal, you need something that will help you get the closeness you want. Below are nine ways to redirect your energy to:

1.    Participation: We can get an enormous amount of satisfaction from life by participating as much as possible getting involved with life.

2.    Helpfulness: Concentrate on being helpful to others while at the same time taking care of yourself. We can attain satisfaction by being valuable to others contributing to the quality of our lives and theirs.

3.    Cooperation: We have no idea yet what can all be done by working together as a team. We must learn to stop pitting man against man. We must quit comparing ourselves against others. We must learn to encourage instead of put down. The following is a quote from one of our clients:

*"After counseling I realized that there were many times that I felt the need to be distant from my wife. It seemed to happen whenever there was a conflict between what she wanted and what I wanted. I decided to work on being more flexible so that I had the ability to not feel so panicky when the situation suggested that I forego what I wanted. I not only discovered that I could survive without getting my way, but I recognized how much I had been missing out on by never allowing the other person to choose our activities. Doing so has added a lot more color to my life."*

4.    Enjoyment: Arrange to get enjoyment from any situation. Whether it be climbing a mountain peak or learning from a failure.

5.  Responsibility: Take responsibility for what you get. If someone is late in keeping an engagement with you, ask yourself, *"What might I have done to make her feel like being late."* Or *"What part of me is like her? Do I keep my commitments?"*

6,  Making yourself happy: You may intellectually believe that you are responsible to make your life happy. But often you don't act like it is your responsibility. Picture this story about going to Heaven in order to make your responsibility clearer:

You die and go to Heaven. You go up that golden escalator and at the top is a big building. You peek in the window and see a lot of very happy people, and decide that is the place you want to be. You knock on the door and someone in a white robe answers and asks, *"Why should we let you in?"*

You answer, *"Because I've been real good and have always done the right thing and I have been better than my husband and better than all of my friends and didn't drink or smoke and I went to church every week."*

The man in the white robe asks, *"Were you happy?"*

You say, *"No. But I was always good."*

He says, *"Good according to who? I can't let anyone in here unless they have learned how to make themselves happy. If you don't know how to do that you might make everyone else unhappy. We can't risk that. Try the place at the bottom of the down escalator. It's a little warm down there, but you'll have a good time because the people there all play your favorite game. They're always trying to prove that they are right and the others are wrong. However, if you ever learn how to make yourself happy, come on back. Then we'd be glad to have you."*

7.  Interest in others: When you no longer need to work so hard to prove yourself you will have time to enjoy being interested in others. Here are some comments from a client:

*"I did some things differently this week. I noticed that I spent more time talking with my wife and I listened to her more. What I used to do was, when she was talking I would be thinking about how I was going to answer her. Now I feel that I can say anything to her without having to figure out how to say it right. If she asks me what I'm thinking, I just answer her honestly."*

8.  Sharing: Share yourself with others. Some people tell you about themselves and it becomes very boring because they are blaming others for what has happened to them. Or they are making alibis for where they are in life. That is not sharing. Sharing is when you tell someone about yourself in a way that they can learn from you. For example consider these two conversations:

*"Boy it is so hard to get baby-sitters in this neighborhood. Kids these days they're not interested in making money. They're more interested in partying."*

*"I was having a hard time finding a baby-sitter. So I asked myself, 'Why am I making this so difficult?" Then I realized that really didn't want to go to the party. I told Eric that I didn't want to go. So, instead, we got a baby-sitter and went out to dinner with some friends."*

The first example is blaming. The second example allows her friend to see her imperfections and learn from her experience.

9.  Finding a purpose: Having a purpose for life is an essential ingredient to leading a fulfilling life. Not having a purpose is like going to a grocery store

213

without deciding what you want. You wander up and down the aisles. Sometimes you have to back track because you realize you needed something from an aisle you've already been down. When you get home you become aware of the item you forgot. As a result you feel dissatisfied and frustrated. Life is like that. If you don't have a sense of direction, you wander aimlessly feeling unsatisfied.

Occasionally, not having a goal is the result of errors in your life style.

One woman came to counseling because she was attracting men who only wanted a brief affair.

When she was younger, she wanted to have a horse. Her parents agreed to buy her one if she could arrange a place to keep it. At the last minute the place where she was going to keep the horse was sold. She was very disappointed and told her parents. They responded by saying only, *"Well, perhaps another time."* She went to a field and cried because she felt her parents didn't care.

In counseling she recognized that she, as a child, decided, *"I must never really WANT anything or I'll risk feeling the pain of rejection from the others who don't care."*

She then recognized that when dating, she never showed the man that she really wanted him. No wonder she always attracted men who didn't want to get involved!

Many people who do not have coals for their life seek satisfaction through useless or destructive ways. For example:

Angie lived with her husband and three children. She felt unfulfilled as a housewife. She started having affairs with other men. She found this extremely exciting. The affairs at least gave her some kind of satisfaction. But she never really felt happy and often felt guilty. During counseling we asked her what she thought was needed in the community. Her answer was, *"more support for parents."*

With encouragement, she decided to lead a study group to provide that service. She found it exciting to watch her group feel better about themselves and their families. Along with some other suggestions in counseling and finding a purpose, she felt no desire to continue having affairs because she now felt worthwhile and satisfied with herself.

But what IS the meaning of life? Only you can answer that question. What is meaningful to one person may not be important to another. Two questions that you might ask yourself in order to find an answer are:

From YOUR perspective what is one thing that would make this world a better place to live?

And with your abilities, how could you contribute to that purpose? Here is an example of how one of our clients answered those questions.

Meaning of life: *"In my opinion, the best way for people to get what they want is through learning how to cooperate."*

My purpose is: *"To learn and to teach others cooperation skills."*

My one-year goals are: *"Take an assertiveness course. Take a leadership training course."*

My five-year goals are: *"Teach my own class on cooperation skills."*

Lifetime goals: *"I would like to write a book on that topic."*

Your goals may be to get your child to stop whining, become known as an honest mechanic, become mayor of your city, or anything that inspires you. There are no correct answers to the above questions. Your answers may vary from month to month or they may last a lifetime. It doesn't matter, as long as you have a focus. It is not important to set rigid goals and keep them. It is important that you develop a sense of direction.

You may want to answer the questions, try them out for a day or a week, see how it feels and then modify them.

Now that you have made your goals, it is helpful to develop a sense of commitment to them. By commitment, we mean giving it your all. (Not a feeling of obligation to see it through.)

To enhance your sense of commitment try this experiment: For ten minutes during the day create thoughts of *"Why bother... Who cares... Nothing I do matters anyway."* The next ten minutes create thoughts of *"What I contribute DOES count. I am a valuable person."*

Which ten minutes made you feel the most alive? A lot of us spend our lives just plodding along, making it through day after day. Having a purpose, setting goals, and being committed makes life more valuable. It's like making an investment. If you haven't invested in the stock market, it's often unimportant to you. But if you've invested in stocks you become extremely interested because you are expecting a return. Life, too requires an investment in order to get a return.

## WHO'S TO BLAME?

Whatever is happening in your life is exactly what you wanted to happen. There is no need to work so hard trying to hide that fact from others because whatever is happening in their lives is exactly what they wanted to happen. Therefore they can't blame you and you can't blame them. We are really all one. ENJOY BEING TOGETHER!

# *The UYO Course*™

## ACTION IS ESSENTIAL

### Do You Express Yourself At 100%?

Many people read the Understanding Yourself & Others book and agree with the principles. They make a lot of sense. However, you may find that they are easy to understand but difficult to apply to the situations in your life.

To make it easier to benefit from these principles we have designed a workshop called the Understanding Yourself & Others Course™. It is a one weekend workshop that helps you live these ideas. It will generate an entirely new level of aliveness in your life.

### HISTORY OF THE UYO™ COURSE

The first time that I taught the Understanding Yourself & Others course™ was in 1971. I was living in Cincinnati, Ohio and had just finished teaching a six week parenting course for a group of 40 people. They requested that I teach them another course to help them improve their personal lives. I then developed the UYO™ course which, at that time consisted of explaining the ideas in this book.

I continued teaching that course until 1981, when we wrote the first edition of this book. After completion of the Understanding Yourself & Others book I decided to redesign the Understanding Yourself & Others course™ into a tool that would actually help people to APPLY the ideas.

At that time I spent months entering data into the computer to find out what was the difference between the clients and students who were able to quickly apply the principles we taught, and the clients and students who thought the ideas were great but could not seem to apply them in their lives.

I went through all of our client and course files and listed all the things we did in our counseling sessions and courses. I then started a process of sorting and re-sorting the data until I was able to recognize a pattern that existed in the work we did with the clients and students who made dramatic and rapid improvement.

We then spent three months designing a course around that pattern. Upon completion we held the first UYO™ course with the new design. There were 16 people in that course. They were so excited about what they received from the program that they brought 63 people to their graduation session. So many people signed up to take the course that we had to schedule two courses a month to accommodate them. Our office was so crowded that we had to move to a place six times as large.

Then people started asking us if we would come to their city to teach a UYO™ course. To accommodate them we started selling franchises. Today we have over fifty Global Relationship Centers throughout the United States and several other countries. To meet the demand we then started an instructor training program and there are now over 500 UYO™ instructors  Our National Headquarters is now located on a 77 acre lakefront training facility in Austin, Texas.

## SPECIAL ATTENTION FOR SPECIAL PEOPLE

One of the things that has made the UYO™ course so popular is that it has been designed to provide special attention for special people. The course is limited to only 24 people. There are two instructors and many assistant instructors. Before attending, each student completes a *"Course Information Sheet"* where you express what you personally want to accomplish to improve your love relationships, work relationships, friendships, or financial position. The instructor team meets prior to the course to study these forms. Your course is basically custom designed to your personal desires. Every course, therefore, is a unique and beautiful experience.

Each student is assigned a *"Guardian Angel"* to continuously monitor their individual progress during the weekend course. There is individual time for each student. Because of the personal attention everyone receives, not only from the instructors, but also from the other students, lasting friendships are formed. I know of no other course that gives so much personal attention!

The course generally starts at 7:00 P.M. on Friday evening and continues  all day Saturday and Sunday. Monday evening there is a graduation celebration. There is then a free follow up session,  and once you have completed the course you may (after additional free training) participate as an assistant at no additional cost.

## A MILLION DOLLAR VALUE!

On several occasions  we have asked UYO™ graduates to make a list of fifteen or twenty things that they have gained from taking the UYO™ course.  After completing their lists we have them assign a dollar value to each item on their list. We have never had anyone's list total less than at least one million dollars. Many items are valued as *"priceless!"*

What is it that makes this program so valuable? Students learn to greatly improve their people skills! They become more understanding. more forgiving, more influential, more loving, more successful and generally happier. They express themselves more accurately and with a new sense of freedom. Within six months, most students report that they have increased their income by at least 20%. They experience more aliveness and they are able to APPLY the things they learned from reading the Understanding Yourself & Others book.

We highly recommend that you enroll in a UYO™ course. Contact Global Relationship Centers National Headquarters at 512-266-3333 for information on the center nearest to you.

# *About the Author*

## Bill Riedler

Bill is owner of Global Relationship Centers, Inc., a personal development business with 50 centers throughout the United States and other countries. He has trained over 500 instructors to teach his many programs, which train thousands each year to improve their people skills, their business skills, their love life their spirituality and their teamwork skills. He has been designing and teaching courses and workshops on personal development since 1963. As you will see if you get the opportunity to meet him he is extremely creative. When he was fourteen he was given a three day battery of tests. Part of the results stated that in terms of creativity, Bill was operating on the genius level. (On the ink blot test he depicted more original perceptions than 99.97% of all the people who had ever taken the test!) We are sure you will find his creativity refreshing when you read his books or participate in the courses he has designed.

## Courses by Global Relationship Centers

Please contact me with information on the Global Relationship Centers programs I have checked below:

❑ **Understanding Yourself & Others™**
A weekend workshop to improve your people skills.

❑ **US Attitudes™**
A course on teamwork skills for individuals and businesses.

❑ **TAGS™ program**
A 12 month, one evening per month continuing education program for UYO™ graduates and there guests.

❑ **The CASH Workshop™**
A four day program for business owners and people who work in sales to improve their cash flow and customer base.

❑ **Enhancing Relationships for Couples™**
A course to increase the intimacy in your love relationship.

❑ **Power TIP Course™**
A course on how to develop POWER Through Inner Peace.

❑ **Your World, Your Camp™**
Kids camp teaching responsibility, esteem and people skills

❑ **Instructor Candidate program**
A two year training to become a UYO™ instructor.

❑ **Owning a Global Relationship Centers Franchise.**

❑ **Send information on the Tape-A-Month Club**

**Complete other side of this form and mail to:**

# GLOBAL
**Relationship
Centers, Inc.**
16101 Stewart Road
Austin, Texas 78734
512-266-3333

Global Relationship Centers

# Book Order Form

❑ **Understanding yourself & Others**
By Bill Riedler          228 pages

Number of copies  ❑                    @ $14.95

plus $1.50 shipping

❑ **Change & Become Yourself**
By Bill Riedler                          32 pages

Number of copies  ❑                    @ $6.95

plus $1.50 shipping

Mail the books ordered above plus information on the programs checked on the other side of this order form to:

Name_____

Address_____

City _____ St._____ Zip_____

Home phone _____

Work phone_____

❑ Enclosed is my check # _____ for $ _____

❑ Please charge my credit card for $ _____

❑ **Visa**   ❑ **Mastercard**   ❑ **Am Express**   ❑ **Discover**

**Card number**_____

**Expiration date** _____

**Signature** _____

# *Notes:*

# *Notes:*

# *Notes:*

# *Notes:*

# *Notes:*